W9-BWM-642

VIETNAM
ON FILM

From THE GREEN BERETS to APOCALYPSE NOW

GILBERT ADAIR

PROTEUS

PROTEUS BOOKS is an imprint of
The Proteus Publishing Group

United States
PROTEUS PUBLISHING CO., INC.
733 Third Avenue
New York, N.Y. 10017
distributed by:
THE SCRIBNER BOOK COMPANIES, INC.
597 Fifth Avenue
New York, N.Y. 10017

United Kingdom
PROTEUS (PUBLISHING) LIMITED
Bremar House,
Sale Place,
London, W2 1PT

ISBN 0 906071 43 7

First published in US 1981

Printed by The Anchor Press Ltd
and Bound by William Brendon & Son Ltd

Book design by Juan Alvarez

Origination by Waterden Reproductions

PICTURE CREDITS

A.F.I./MONUMENT
ALLIED ARTISTS
AMERICAN INTERNATIONAL PICTURES
AMERICAN ZOETROPE
ASSOCIATED ARTISTS
COLUMBIA PICTURES
E.M.I.
EAGLE FILMS
ENTERPRISE PICTURES
METRO GOLDWYN MAYER
PARAMOUNT PICTURES
RAINBOW PICTURES
TWENTIETH CENTURY FOX
UNITED ARTISTS
WARNER BROS
UNIVERSAL PICTURES

THE KOBAL COLLECTION
THE NATIONAL FILM ARCHIVE/STILLS LIBRARY
THE OTHER CINEMA

Acknowledgements to researcher Martin Hitchcock and heartfelt thanks to my editor Nicolas Locke without whom...

Gilbert Adair

CONTENTS

INTRODUCTION

SINCE ALMOST every commentator on Hollywood's treatment of Vietnam has fallen into the admittedly tempting trap of equating the mythology of modern warfare with that of moviemaking — the war 'going over budget' , the problems of 'location shooting' — I may as well put my five cents' worth in at once. While researching this book, I became increasingly puzzled by the major studios' apparent reluctance to come to grips with a subject that, apart from having all but monopolized the various media platforms for national debate, seemed to offer a host of intriguing dramatic possibilities. I was also plagued by an indistinct recollection of some other burning issue that the movie industry had dealt with in equally circumspect fashion. But what could it be? As it happens, it was in a London cinema screening *Apocalypse Now* and made disagreeably steamy by wet umbrellas and crumpled raincoats, that I succeeded in pinning down the elusive parallel: the issue was nudity. Whatever more profound reflections might be occasioned by Coppola's epic, here at last, surely, was the Vietnam war full frontal. Perhaps even its *Deep Throat*.

If that analogy seems offensively frivolous, it's worth recalling that *Hair,* the prototype of counterculture folk art, breached the taboo of nudity on stage to externalize, so to speak, its mildly dissident sentiments. More to the point, Hollywood has sometimes given the impression of curbing its already tentative handling of Vietnam and related themes by a kind of self-imposed censorship remarkably similar in effect to that which had for over three decades frustrated any real advance in its representation of sexuality. This self-censorship, if such it can be described, has only very gradually been relaxed (a few, mostly aberrant exceptions apart, e.g. *The Green Berets).* Firstly, through oblique dialogue references to the war, as was the case in a series of exploitation road movies whose motorcyclist heroes were often vets putting skills learnt in Vietnam to more directly criminal purpose (titles such as *Satan's Sadists, Angels from Hell,* etc). Travis Bickle, eponymous hero of Martin Scorsese's *Taxi Driver* (1976), is also a war veteran; but more significant than the few occasions on which Vietnam is specifically mentioned in the dialogue is a pervasive moral and physical squalor whose reverberations far exceed what would normally be justified by the movie's depiction of Manhattan's seamy underside. Numerous traditional genres were annexed in this way, notably the genial, all-purpose Western which had at least the advantage of a bona fide historical precedent. It frequently served to allegorize the war (e.g. Ralph Nelson's *Soldier Blue,* 1970, a relentlessly brutal denunciation of the Indian massacres, and Robert Aldrich's *Ulzana's Raid,* 1972, whose Apache warriors were turned into blood brothers of the Viet Cong), as did, though at greater violence to narrative credibility, the medieval romance (e.g. John Huston's *A Walk with Love and Death,* 1969). If the studios finally got round to making movies *about* Vietnam, they nevertheless began, by an odd reversal of chronology, with its aftermath, with the reintegration of vets into a society which greeted them as if they had returned from Mars. Or else with the young people who had chosen *en masse* to opt out of that society and fight the war (i.e. its advocates) on home territory — on campus, in demonstrations and even, with the release of *The Green Berets* in 1968, outside movie theaters.

Though the best of these efforts can be defended as worthy and well-intentioned, in general the subject matter proved too complex, too multilayered to be comfortably confined within the closed plot structures — a beginning, middle and end in that order — that were natural to the American cinema, and the results more often ran the gamut from the queasily ambivalent to the downright dishonest. It seemed almost the fun thing to be against the war if it meant filling the screen with sit-ins, peace-ins and love-ins in Death Valley, with all the psychedelic paraphernalia of the protest movement. And it was much more fun attacking America than defending Vietnam. The Star-Spangled Banner, even when unfurled to ironic effect, is still a jazzy, brightly colored icon. A hideously maimed child is somehow less invigorating.

I was reminded of this when I attended a screening of several short films — polemically pro-Vietnam — by the distinguished Cuban director, Santiago Alvarez (*Hanoi, Tuesday 13, April in Vietnam in the Year of the Cat, The Stampede).* The predominantly under thirties audience, of impeccable liberal credentials, were respectfully attentive to these heartening if harrowing documentaries, but one sensed that the angel of boredom, though it had not yet settled on the auditorium, was hovering dangerously near at hand. Then his *LBJ* was shown, a scurrilously witty collage of anti-Americana, in the director's own words "a satirical pamphlet in three chapters" in which the letters of the Presidential monogram also stood for, respectively, Luther King, Bob and John F. Kennedy. Suddenly the house was alert, practically hissing the villians and hooting at the more flagrant examples of doublespeak perpetrated by some of them. But when this in turn was followed by *79 Springs,* a straightforward tribute to Ho Chi Minh and the resilience of the Vietnamese people, as one man we all sank back into our former lethargic earnestness.

Thus the products born of Hollywood's brief idyll — or rather, marriage of convenience — with 60s youth tended to reveal more of the period's contradictions in their trappings than in their ostensible 'substance'; and it's indicative of the relatively marginal status of Vietnam as the raw material of fiction that the most commercially successful of all youth-oriented movies, George Lucas's *American Graffiti* (1973), turned its back on the war altogether and set its affectionate celebration of adolescent mores unashamedly in the Eisenhower era. So that of the two opposing axes of received wisdom concerning the subject of this book (and which were tirelessly communicated to me while I was writing it) — (I) that there are too few Vietnam movies to warrant a full-length study and (2) that every American feature film made during the decade of 1965-75 must directly or indirectly reflect some aspect of its political makeup and therefore be relevant to the debate — both may be said to contain elements of truth.

The period covered is that which stretches approximately from *The Green Berets* to *Apocalypse Now* (although a handful of movies predate the former and already, since the latter was completed, we have seen Milos Forman's adaptation of *Hair,* in which the first signs of Vietnam nostalgia may be detected). I have preferred to concentrate almost exclusively on works of fiction, as I believe them to offer up a far richer vein of ideology than documentaries, which in any case have never loomed very large in Hollywood's history. Similarly, I have not dwelt on non-American films.

This has, of course, no pretensions to being a book on the Vietnam war. But if I were asked to define its ambition beyond that of mere documentation, I might refer to one last personal reminiscence. In 1972, at the height of the so-called Christmas bombing of North Vietnam, I was discussing the war with a few friends. One of them, in a frank admission of apathy, made the whimsical comment that he had more interest in, "put more faith" in, say, the moon than in Vietnam, because he could *see* the moon but he couldn't see Vietnam. Though in many respects a perfectly idiotic observation, I've found it to be a naggingly memorable one. And, after all, during one of the most turbulent periods of American history, when a gulf opened between much of the population and the nation's ideologists that has not closed since, Hollywood continued blithely to put its faith in the moon (in the trivially romantic sense that it rhymes with 'June'). Like the dog that attracted Sherlock Holmes' attention by *not* barking, it's perhaps the very absence of movies that is most deserving of study.

SECTION I

APOCALYPSE THEN

IN THIS century, the United States has been involved in four major wars: World Wars I and II, Korea and Vietnam. In 1918, the year World War I ended and only one year after America had intervened, D. W. Griffith, the director of *The Birth of a Nation* (1915) and *Intolerance* (1916), made his first movie on the subject, *Hearts of the World,* a melodrama so blatantly anti-German in attitude as to cause, in Erich von Stroheim's words, "hundreds and thousands of men and women in more or less pro-German audiences in the United States to have a complete change of heart". Thereafter the trenches, bunkers and twisted barbed wire, the imagery by which World War I is instantly recognizable on the screen, became a familiar feature of Hollywood movies for the next two decades.

By the mid-30s, however, another World War was all too noisily in the offing; and both before and after America's intervention in the wake of the Japanese assault on Pearl Harbor, the World War II movie became almost an autonomous genre whose popularity, eclipsing that of the war movie *per se,* has remained constant to the present day. In June 1950, North Korean troops crossed the 38th Parallel and invaded the Republic of Korea. A few days later, when his call for a cease fire had been ignored, President Truman decided to send in American naval and air forces. In September of the same year, a delegation of Hollywood notables was dispatched to the White House to acquaint the President with the

'HEARTS OF THE WORLD' *Directed by D.W. Griffith.*

industry's unanimous support (unanimous, that is, except for those directors, writers and actors who had been blacklisted by their own colleagues following the very American activities of Senator McCarthy's UnAmerican Activities Committee). They declared notably that: "We are at your service, at the service of the country and the United Nations." Although, for various reasons, fewer movies were made about Korea than about the preceding World Wars, those which did surface (mostly B-movies like Samuel Fuller's *The Steel Helmet,* 1950) were serenely untroubled by any doubts or disillusionment concerning the American initiative.

And then came Vietnam. It's a delicate matter picking over the ruins to try and locate the precise moment when the Americans first opened fire in Indochina, for the war's origins were all but obscured by the ebbing tide of French colonialism (since 1953 heavily subsidized by the United States), but it is on record that by 1968, the year of *The Green Berets,* co-directed by Ray Kellogg and its star John Wayne, their forces in the region already totalled almost half a million men. Though a commercial success in countries whose geographical proximity to the war made them particularly sensitive to its outcome, such as Australia and Japan, as well as in certain hinterland areas of the United States with a high recruitment rate, the South and Midwest, the release of *The Green Berets* was also the signal for widespread demonstrations — the picketing and even bombing of movie theaters exhibiting it — and a merciless critical drubbing. Since then every movie reflecting even marginally the American presence in Vietnam has been greeted as some sort of event and the merest hint of ideological revisionism in its dialogue pounced upon.

To understand why Hollywood was so chary of depicting the Vietnam war within a conventional gung ho framework, it will be necessary to give brief consideration to its treatment of those which preceded it. World War I, in a sense, was not an 'American' affair at all. In 1914, with President Wilson determined to pursue a "Keep Out" policy, the United States was prey to another of its frequent but never very durable bouts of pacifist isolationism, as witness movie titles like *Be Neutral, Neutrality* and *War Is Hell.* Those rare movies which sought to transcend such cautious abstractions and make what was happening in Europe come alive in terms of plot and character motivation were generally obliged to set the action in one of those reassuringly unspecified countries where over the years so many fictional wars — in novels, plays and films — have been waged to symbolic effect. Thus Herbert Brenon's *War Brides (1916),* with the arrestingly surnamed tragedienne Alla Nazimova playing a young wife who, when her husband is killed in action, refuses to obey a royal decree ordering widows to remarry and bear more children to carry on the war (which, if such long-term planning is any indication, promised to be a somewhat lengthy engagement).

*Poster – **'ALL QUIET ON THE WESTERN FRONT'***

If geopolitical frontiers remained undefined, however, the enemy had to be particularized at least to the degree of their not resembling Americans — or rather, white Anglo-Saxon Protestant Americans. Since all other signs of national status had been piously expunged, this could only be achieved through racial typification. In both *War Brides* and Thomas Ince's prestigious superproduction, *Civilization* (1916), the brutal soldiery are inescapably Teutonic in appearance. Ince's film, which involves a young submarine engineer whose body is invested by the spirit of Christ and put to higher service in the crusade against war, had an ostensibly pacifist premise. But by again locating the origin of the war in question — and, by implication, the origin of War itself — in a thinly disguised racial type, it cunningly insinuated the urgent necessity for taking action against what was presented as an incorrigibly bellicose nation. Its 'neutrality' was so patently biased, in fact, that Sweden, a country which was truly neutral, banned its importation.

German Infantryman (Lew Ayres) tends a wounded enemy after a battle in no-man's land – ***'ALL QUIET ON THE WESTERN FRONT'***

In these films, released concurrently with the war in Europe but prior to American intervention, we can already see taking shape a mythologizing process which was to suffer very little change in the decades to come. Once and for all, as far as the movie industry was concerned, this was a 'futile', 'tragic' war in which 'the flower of youth was lost on the field of Flanders', and so forth. More than any other, it seemed to lend itself to a vaguely mystical pacifism. So much so that certain directors were apparently unaware of any contradiction in using it as the backdrop for an anti-war tract between filming two conventionally heroic Boys' Own Adventure movies about World War II.

Gregory Peck stars in Lewis Milestone's ***'PORK CHOP HILL'***

A case in point is Lewis Milestone, who made his reputation with the celebrated, Oscar-winning *All Quiet on the Western Front* (1930), from Erich Maria Remarque's best-selling novel. Though overrated in its day, *All Quiet* remains a moving indictment of the waste and stupidity inherent in all wars, however 'just'. The fact that the story is told from the enemy's point of view, with the doomed young German soldiers being played by attractive American actors, not only humanizes its sometimes ponderous didacticism but also makes it more difficult for nationalistic considerations to come into play. Far better than the spurious universality gained by setting the movie on some purely symbolic battleground, such a casting *parti pris* succeeds in blurring our sense of two opposing sides locked in combat and exposes the condition of war itself. This 'fraternization', so to speak, of American actors and German soldiers mirrors that which took place in the trenches during the Christmas truce of 1914 and encourages the spectator to identify emotionally with characters who are often — and in war movies, invariably — categorized as aliens, bearing all the racial, social and cultural stigmata of incurable 'otherness'. Its unforgettable last image of the young German hero (Lew Ayres) stretching out his hand to stroke a butterfly and suddenly convulsing in death from a sniper's bullet makes the naive but affecting statement that aspirations toward beauty and nature have never been the sole prerogative of 'our boys', that Germans too are human, every mother's son of them.

As Milestone's career advanced, however, it became clear that his pacifist convictions were by no means immutable. He was quite prepared to discard them, for example, in *The Purple Heart* (1944), a straightforward guts 'n' glory World War II movie marred by a crudely racist treatment of the Japanese, and *Pork Chop Hill* (1959), ditto for Korea. British actor Richard Attenborough, a below-decks veteran of innumerable morale boosting war films, launched his career as a director with an allstar adaptation of Charles Chilton and Joan Littlewood's satirical anti-war musical *Oh What a Lovely War* (1969), then coolly proceeded to film *A Bridge Too Far* (1978), a spectacular reconstruction of the battle of Arnhem for which many of the same stars were required to pull their tongues out of their cheeks and restiffen their upper lips in preparation for another 'big push'.

It would be easy to attribute such ideological volte faces to sheer mercenary opportunism. To be sure, movies are made to make money and anti-war movies doubtless get made because their producers reckon them to be what the public wants at that particular moment. But beyond these economic facts of life (which apply to fully one hundred percent of Hollywood film-

Richard Attenborou
'OH! WHAT A LOV
WAR'** and **'A BRID
TOO FAR'

making) it's probable that, whenever an anti-war story was mooted around the studios, the decision to give it a World War I setting was taken at an almost subliminal level. (There are too many examples to list here, though mention should be made of Kubrick's *Paths of Glory,* 1958, and Losey's *King and Country,* 1964. The exceptions mostly centered on colorful tête-à-tête skirmishes between stylish air aces who 'respected each other' and managed to preserve a cavalryesque sense of chivalry high above the carnage, as in John Guillermin's *The Blue Max,* 1966, and Corman's *Von Richtofen and Brown,* GB *The Red Baron,* 1971).

This semi-automatic concordance of theme and period can be accounted for by a combination of factors: the tragically arbitrary set of events which led to the outbreak of war; the monotony of its strategy, with both Allied and German forces dug in along a line stretching from the Baltic to the Mediterranean; the stark contrast between the insouciance with which the first Tommies left for France, persuaded that they would be home for Christmas, and the hideous reality confronting them in the trenches; the unglamorous nature of the fighting and wholescale slaughter of its major battles; the disastrous diplomatic aftermath; and, not least, the widely held belief that it constituted a turning point in history, with the concomitant nostalgia for a Belle Epoque already viewed through the soft focus of memory.

World War II presented a substantially different picture. If World War I had been exclusively a game of chance, here apparently was a game of skill with plenty of opportunities (for the filmmaker, that is) to move freely over the board. From jungle combat in the Philippines and Pacific Islands to air strikes over the Rhine, from a North African campaign waged against the

*Alan Arkin, as the determinedly deranged Yossarian – **'CATCH 22'**. Directed by Mike Nichols.*

gallant 'good German' Field-Marshal Rommel to undercover activity in the Balkans, it was for Hollywood's purposes a tourist's war with no shortage of local color for the romantic interludes. It was a relief, too, that the moral and political issues seemed so clear-cut. In the face of an aggressor as monstrous as Hitler, pacifism was, as it were, disarmed – tarred with the inglorious brush of 'appeasement'. For once all shades of opinion concurred in the necessity for taking up arms. And this solidarity is reflected in the relative good humor and optimism of many World War II movies (generally perceived by their audiences, even after the period when they were considered an integral part of the war effort, as upbeat entertainments), which were only slightly affected by the postwar revelation of the full extent of Nazi atrocities.

If a few directors had the courage to tackle the highly uncommercial subject of concentration camps (e.g. Stanley Kramer in *Judgment at Nuremberg,* 1961), for the majority — as for many an ex-soldier who had enjoyed a 'good' war — they were oddly detachable from the main event. Nothing in the unproblematic heroics of a film like J. Lee Thompson's *The Guns of Navarone* (1961), to take one example from among hundreds, suggested that its fictional fortress belonged to the same war that had spawned Lidice and Auschwitz.

As mentioned above, the World War II movie soon became almost a separate genre, encompassing without too much strain

Middle class English bravery from Greer Garson and Walter Pidgeon in the World War II epic ***'MRS MINIVER'***

such varied approaches as the farcical *(1941)*, satirical *(Catch-22)*, black comedy (Lubitsch's *To Be Or Not To Be)*, musical (the 1943 version of *The Desert Song)*, romantic (the remake of *The Four Horsemen of the Apocalypse)*, adventure *(The Great Escape)*, psychological *(The Young Lions)*, melodramatic *(From Here To Eternity)*, sentimental *(Mrs. Miniver)*, biographical *(Patton, G.B. Patton - Lust for Glory)* semidocumentary *(Tora! Tora! Tora!)* and even, though generally long after hostilities had ceased, pacifist (notably David Lean's *The Bridge On the River Kwai*, 1957, from Pierre Boulle's novel). On the other hand, John Huston's *Let There Be Light*, a documentary on the psychological rehabilitation of shell-shocked GIs, is to the present day banned from public exhibition by the War Department which had commissioned it back in 1948. Another of Huston's documentaries, *The Battle of San Pietro* (1944), focusing on the struggle of one infantry division for a key Italian village, was cut by a third because of its allegedly ambivalent attitude toward the army's morale, a trace of which may still be found in the suggestion of its commentary (spoken by the director himself) that there were to be "many more San Pietros, a thousand more, and many of those you see here alive will die". Certain sequences of Delmer Daves' excellent *Pride of the Marines* (1945), which dealt with the difficult readjustment to civilian life of a blinded Marine (John

Air attack by The AICHI (val) strike force – ***'TORA! TORA! TORA!'***

Garfield), were so painfully realistic and the subject as a whole so grim that Warner's publicity department attempted to mislead the public with a poster whose understandably forced cheerfulness contrived to suggest a bright romantic comedy!

In some respects — precisely those which made it so conducive to cinematic re-enactment — World War II was uncharacteristic of modern warfare. If one didn't look too searchingly, good and evil appeared encased in the simple black-and-white symmetries of a chessboard. Advances in military technology permitted a liberty of movement which totally reversed the helpless stalemate of World War I without the attendant frustration, as would later be the case in Vietnam, of sitting on a useless pile of nuclear weaponry while getting bogged down in a kind of tactical fighting for which the enemy was far better trained. Such is the period's enduring popularity — extending to novels, TV shows, comic strips, toys, fashions, even the perverse boom in Nazi memorabilia — that if a war movie is mentioned, we immediately suppose it to be about World War II. In spite of concentration camps, the saturation bombing of Dresden and Coventry and atomic razing of Hiroshima and Nagasaki, thought of it seems to conjure up no especial horrors in the average person's mind. Perhaps conditioned by numerous celebrations of American derring-do, British muddling through, French cunning and, for comic relief, Italian incompetence, succeeding generations have been anesthetized to its more terrifying realities. Like the Western, it has become a source of myths, sustained by its own set of endearingly predictable stereotypes: the Gestapo with their sinister granny glasses, their black leather trench coats and their "Ve haf vays of making you talk" , the tight-lipped commander briefing his men on a mission with a brisk "Some of you may not come back alive...", etc. And most dramatizations of World War II bear as much resemblance to the real event as most Westerns do to the real Old West.

As long as the war was being waged in Europe, Hollywood

Alec Guinness, as the C.O. of concentration camp internees, takes it on the chin from his Japanese adversary – ***'BRIDGE ON THE RIVER KWAI'***

could revel shamelessly in the opportunities it provided for high adventure, but its chronic incapacity to come to terms with defeat, its need to disguise it rather than — like the British at Dunkirk — glory in it, proved a major stumbling block in filming the Pacific war. Although the degree to which Pearl Harbor might be considered a 'victory' for the Japanese was compromised by their failure to officialize the assault by declaring war in advance, there could be no question that it was a defeat for the United States. Within ninety minutes, eight battleships, three light cruisers and four miscellaneous vessels had been sunk or seriously damaged and almost two hundred aeroplanes, more than half America's air power on the island, had been destroyed. In addition, 2400 Americans were killed and about as many injured, a casualty list whose public release was long delayed to avert a national panic. Roosevelt instantly declared war, but American momentum had suffered a crucial setback and a series of military reverses followed in Bataan, Corregidor and Wake Island.

The G.I's come out on top in Sam Fuller's Korean based ***'FIXED BAYONETS'***

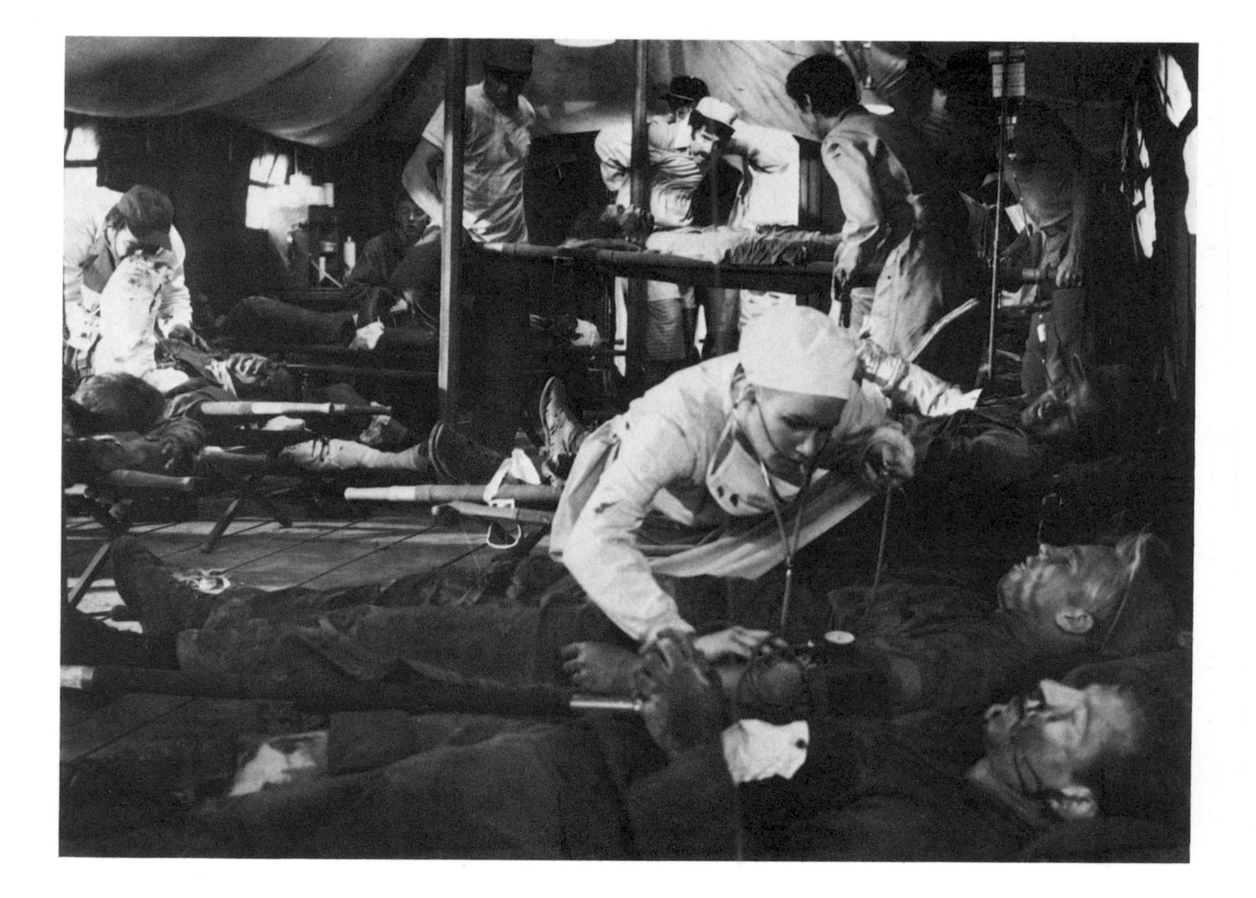

Altman's satire ***'M*A*S*H'.*** *Major 'Hot Lips' (Sally Kellerman) checks pulses, watched by Trapper John (Elliott Gould).*

This unnerving start to the war had a powerfully galvanizing effect on Middle American prejudices. Southern California, for example, 'discovered' to its horror that it had been harboring a considerable Japanese-American population, both Issei (first generation) and Nisei (their offspring), who were — unfortunately for them — infallibly detectable in any crowd. All at once they found themselves the target of homegrown retaliation. Apart from the petty harassment which they had to endure from racially 'pure' Americans (and ethnic minorities not implicated by association in the country's disgrace) — restaurants refusing to serve them or insurance policies summarily canceled — a warrant was issued by Earl Warren, the reputedly liberal Attorney-General of California, authorizing the roundup of such 'aliens' and their transportation to other states. Opposition to these measures was duly made by the American Civil Liberties Union but proved totally ineffective. Henceforth 'Japs' were portrayed in war movies as congenitally malevolent beings only a few rungs up the biological scale from vermin, their traditional facial inscrutability transformed by heavy underlighting into cruel masks of atheistic inhumanity. Even their inexplicable indifference to the virginal charms of American womanhood — so untypical of 'the enemy' — somehow counted as a point against them.

This image was more or less fixed for the next thirty years (almost the only sympathetic portrayals of Japanese in the American cinema of the period were Marlon Brando's interpreter in Daniel Mann's *The Teahouse of the August Moon,*1956, and Alec Guinness's businessman in Mervyn LeRoy's *A Majority of One,* 1962) and would moreover serve indiscriminately for Koreans, Chinese and, in a few notorious instances, Vietnamese. In Leo McCarey's abysmal *Satan Never Sleeps* (1962 , GB *The Devil Never Sleeps),* a ludicrously implausible melodrama of American missionaries in the Far East, the Chinese protagonist is grossly caricatured so long as he remains a rabid communist. Turned capitalist in embryo after a lightning conversion, he miraculously becomes (in McCarey's mind, at least) natural, likeable and, in short, a regular guy.

One of the consequences of South-East Asia's progressive Communization from the 40s to the 70s has been, in a certain knee-jerk mentality, the sublimation of ideology by race, the determination to identify Communism and its spread exclusively with 'barbaric' Asian peoples (among which, of course, are included the Russians). In fact, the attitude of right-minded Americans toward Communism has always been fundamentally *racist* in nature, fueled by rhetoric no less hysterical in its irrationality than the crudest anti-black or anti-Semitic rabble-rousing. If in the mythology of the Ku Klux Klan Communists have never challenged the supremacy of blacks as embodiments of 'racial' degeneracy, it can only be because the latter are rather more in evidence in the Deep South. For Commie haters, however, the abusive term 'red' is conveniently color-oriented, while the even more derisory 'pinko' (to designate fellow travelers) evokes the ambiguous status of the half-caste. Polemical literature on the

Hawkeye (Donald Sutherland) plots, over breakfast with Lt. Dish (Jo Ann Pflug). Col. Henry Blake (Roger Bowen) standing.

subject (in particular, the speeches of the Republican Party's lunatic fringe) has always tended to portray Communism as a plague, a mysteriously contagious malady which, having been allowed to reach epidemic proportions over much of the globe (the celebrated 'domino theory'), must at all costs be halted before it contaminates healthy Americans. So just as Communist states make it hard for their citizens to get out, the United States makes it hard for a Communist to get in. Visitors risk having their visas annulled if suspected of 'smuggling in' the dreaded ideology.

But ideology is precisely what has been drained from such demagoguery. What the majority of Americans hold in abhorrence is less the theoretical foundations of Marxist-Leninism, of which they are largely ignorant, than its most disheartening social realities: the Gulags, of course, but also — and perhaps more acutely — the terrifying drabness of life behind the Iron Curtain, the shortage of material goods, *the absence of neon.* Both capitalism and Communism impinge on the American psyche in terms of hardware: on the one hand, glossy consumerism which is by its very nature conspicuous; on the other, those ghastly East Berlin streets just glimpsed beyond the Brandenburg Gate. Never was the grass greener on *this* side of the fence. And when, with the Korean war, this irrational fear was grafted onto another — the deep-seated fear inspired by marauding, mosquito-like hordes of Asians — it was evident that paranoia would soon have a whole nation in its clammy grip.

Mark Andrews (Burt Reynolds) and Denise Dalbert (Danielle Allbry) with gook trouble – ***'OPERATION CIA'***

Brock (Gene Barry) Goldie (Nat 'King' Cole) et al in Sam Fuller's ***'CHINA GATE'***

The outbreak of hostilities in Korea was, of course, preceded (rather like the 'pre-echo' on a record) by an extended period of 'phoney war' with global Communism. After Germany's surrender in 1945 the Soviet Army, entrenched halfway across Europe, had remained more or less on a war footing, with emphasis in the current Five Year Plan abruptly switched from consumer goods back to armaments. In a famous speech in Fulton, Missouri, Churchill coined the term 'Iron Curtain'. And when in February 1947 Truman got the backing of Congress to send 400 million dollars worth of economic and military aid to Greece and Turkey, countries devastated by the war and threatening to 'go over' to the other side, it amounted to a declaration of the Cold War (of which the 80s have seen a resurgence: Cold War II?). As Communism, however, was widely perceived as something so elusive, formless and insidious that, despite the Government's increasingly hawkish foreign policy, it might yet worm its evil way into the national consciousness, this war had to be fought — from the Middle American point of view — no less vigilantly on the domestic front.

The McCarthy period, the trials and hearings, the Friendly and Unfriendly Witnesses, the apotheosis of the Fifth Amendment, have all been sufficiently, even exhaustively documented in case-studies and memoirs to need recounting here. But though, in relation to the lasting historical significance of the larger context, undue attention has been paid to the glamorous but relatively marginal Hollywood hearings as well as to the 'Ten' — directors and screenwriters who refused to bow under pressure and perjure themselves — they are crucial to any understanding of the cagily obeisant posture adopted by most Hollywood moguls at the time. If from no other source, this can be gauged from the profound embarrassment of Sam Goldwyn at having produced — back in 1943 when the USA and USSR enjoyed an uneasy alliance — a Lillian Hellman scripted pro-Russia movie, *The North Star* (directed by the decidedly versatile Lewis Milestone), or of MGM at having financed an idiotic melodrama directed by Gregory Ratoff the following year, *Song of Russia,* whose harmless iconography was, in any case, far more indebted to a pre-Soviet mythology of balalaikas, lyrical embraces in cornfields and the opening chords of Tchaikovsky's First Piano Concerto.

French demonstrators under the eyes of the military in Vietnam – ***'LOST COMMAND'***

When war broke out in Korea, therefore, Hollywood producers would tread an exceptionally wary path, conscious that shifting allegiances might easily cause the most candidly patriotic effort subsequently to rebound in their faces. Not that there was any shortage of product — war has traditionally been good news both for movie production and attendances — but few major directors cared to venture into such uncharted, booby-trapped territory. (To be sure, Ford — as later for Vietnam — made a documentary, *This is Korea,* in 1951.) Also, in view of the undiminished favor enjoyed by World War II movies, the industry was loath to become enmeshed in a whole new war, one for which it, like the rest of the nation, had been totally unprepared. This caution was redoubled when, in spite of General MacArthur's notoriously rash forecast (as old as war itself) that it would all be over by Christmas, the American forces were utterly trounced by the Koreans in the first two months of fighting. Or when, with MacArthur's controversial dismissal by Truman in the dark winter of 1950/1, the war lost the only larger-than-life 'hero' it could ever lay claim to.

If the very first Korean War movie, Samuel Fuller's *The Steel Helmet* (shot largely in Hollywood's Griffith Park on a budget of just over 100,000 dollars), had all the rough edges of Poverty Row cheeseparing, it benefitted at least from Fuller's own brand of demonic energy and refreshing lack of hypocrisy (Fuller is right-wing and doesn't care who knows it). Thereafter, it was downhill most of the way. An indifferent string of movies followed, dealing

Aftermath of Vietminh bombing in Saigon – ***'THE QUIET AMERICAN'***

with the war either literally (the best of these being again by Fuller, *Fixed Bayonets,* 1951) or metaphorically (as with the weird if not quite wonderful sci-fi allegory, *Red Planet Mars,* directed by Harry Horner in 1952), all of which will have to be packed into the same tight footnote to cinema history.

What is interesting about them, however — especially with regard to the first halting attempts to chronicle America's involvement in Indochina — is that Hollywood seems to have proceeded on the complacent assumption that Korea was merely a coda to World War II, whereas it can now be seen as a full-scale dress-rehearsal for Vietnam. Here, as would later happen, American soldiers were fighting a semi-guerilla army in a remote country and for a dubious cause: the immediate welfare of the United States had not been and could not conceivably be imperilled by North Korea. Here, too, they would find themselves gatecrashing a local conflict with North pitted against South. Here, too, atrocities relating to the treatment of prisoners or civilians suspected of sheltering the enemy would be recorded on both sides. And finally, to paraphrase MacArthur's famous epitaph for old soldiers, this war, like the one to come, never actually *ended,* it just faded away in inconclusive peace talks and a solution that satisfied no-one.

The U.S. Ambassador (Marlon Brando) and his wife (Sandra Church) escape Communist insurgents – ***'THE UGLY AMERICAN'***

Last minute instructions before the air assault to save Dien Bien Phu – ***'JUMP INTO HELL'***

Perhaps for this reason American opinion has never come to grips with the meaning of Korea: as an event, it has remained *illegible.* If Vietnam was to polarize sympathies to such a degree that even the most mind-numbing adventure movies were obliged to pay lip service to at least some of the issues at stake (e.g. David Janssen's 'liberal' journalist in *The Green Berets)*, then Korea, except for those directly involved, passed as in a bad dream — one not sufficiently nightmarish to wake the sleeper. And Hollywood both fostered and slavishly reflected this indifference by turning out a ragbag of duds which —if the spectator half-closed his eyes — could be mistaken for being about World War II. Indeed, the best-known film to be set in Korea is undoubtedly Robert Altman's *M*A*S*H** (1970), whose spaced-out irreverence and callously anarchistic high jinks make it about Vietnam in all but place-names. Even if the characters never smoke pot, one has the distinct impression that the director does.

The real Vietnam had — on film — a singularly undistinguished prehistory. A handful of long forgotten B-movie titles: *Saigon* (with Alan Ladd and Veronica Lake), *A Yank in Indo China, A Yank in Viet-Nam* (how that hyphen dates it!), *Operation CIA,* the regulation shocker from Samuel Fuller, *China Gate;* and Mark Robson's clumsy apologia of the French involvement, *The Lost Command.* Considerably more ambitious than the two *Yanks* were a duo of *Americans:* Joseph L. Mankiewicz's *The Quiet American* (1958), which 'corrected' Graham Greene's novel by transforming its protagonist (not so ironically played by World War II's 'most decorated soldier', Audie Murphy) from a dangerous *naif* into a Communist-betrayed innocent; and George Englund's *The Ugly American* (1962, from the novel by William J. Lederer and Eugene Burdick), a muddled political tract set a trifle conspicuously in a mythical South-East Asian state named Sarkhan and remembered only, if at all, for Marlon Brando as its American ambassador in natty striped pants, silk topper and Ronald Colman moustache.

The war itself, when everyone had stood back, taken their pipes out of their mouths and agreed there was one, appeared to offer unlimited opportunities to the filmmaker: the pacifist slant of World War I, the high adventure of World War II, the Communist conspiracy of Korea, even a dramatically troubled aftermath recalling that of the Civil War (for this was also a civil war, no less in the States than in Vietnam, with Kent State as a domestic My Lai). And yet, as I hope to show, Hollywood didn't simply pass the buck, it tried to bury it. As the unprofessionally fumbling entertainments officer in *M*A*S*H** might have put it over his loudspeaker: "Thrills and spills with the... the fighting men of the Green Berets. See our boys... um, see our boys claw their way to... to... victory. I mean... Sorry, that should read 'defeat' — claw their way to defeat... With a cast of thousands in, er... in *The Vietnam War.* Tonight!"

Summary execution —
'FIVE GATES TO HELL'

SECTION II
GUTS 'N' GLORY

THERE IS a scene in *Holocaust,* the television dramatization of the Hitlerian 'final solution', in which the young Jewish hero, hiding in a ditch, is witness to the massacre of 40,000 of his fellow concentration camp internees. The series had its fair share both of defenders and detractors — the English dramatist and critic Dennis Potter referred contemptuously to Jews being "boiled down into soap opera" — but few commentators paused to reflect on the unwieldy logistics of genocide, even when considered solely in filmic terms. How, for a start, does one actually depict the killing of 40,000 people? Assuming that one has at one's disposal a cast of 40,000 (an improbable eventuality), how does one simulate their massacre without either boring the spectator, not exactly unused to small-screen violence, or encouraging him into a kind of vicarious complicity with the thrilling excesses of Nazi sadism?

The quite reasonable solution arrived at by the show's writers or director was: through the eyes of an observer. But here, too, an unforseeable problem of dramatic representation arises. On what resources of talent and experience can an actor, be he the world's greatest, call in order to register horror so profound as to be commensurate with its supposed object? In this particular episode of *Holocaust,* the actor in question proved competent enough — the pupils of his eyes dilated convincingly, his mouth gaped open in incredulity — but in no way could he be said to have 'risen to the occasion' of the crime. Had he been watching an automobile accident, the assassination of a President or an oversized primate scaling the Empire State building with a blonde clutched to its chest, his facial reaction would not have been appreciably different. But, like the threat of nuclear extinction, Nazi death camps offer such a difference in *degree* of horror from anything that preceded them that it has become almost a difference in *kind.* What is therefore required of such fiction-producing factories as television and Hollywood, when dealing with this subject-matter, is that they contrive to distance themselves not only from the material but also from their own time-honored systems of narrative codes: otherwise, the results will only be grotesque. Though the idea of such light comedians as Cary Grant and Ginger Rogers at loose in war-ravaged Europe may be, within the Hollywood context, acceptable enough, their presence in a concentration camp, as in Leo McCarey's *Once Upon a Honeymoon,* is deeply offensive — or would be if it weren't so ludicrous. (In fairness to the film, however, it should be noted that in 1942, when it was made, the term 'concentration camp' had yet to acquire genocidal connotations).

Transportation for Meryl Streep's Jewish husband, played by James Wood, in N.B.C.'s ***'HOLOCAUST'***

Since it was too much to hope that the first Vietnam-related movies would subject the confused political background of the war to any real scrutiny or analysis, criticizing them for failing to do so is a futile exercise. Not that a movie like *The Green Berets* is apolitical: on the contrary, it assumes its Neanderthal hawkish stance far less guardedly than most 'liberal' movies — whether or not about Vietnam — assume theirs. Moreover, it would be naive to write off John Wayne, as some apologists have managed to do, as a political 'innocent': the ignorance of these so-called 'innocents' has a habit of steering them straight into the camp of extreme reaction (e.g. Ezra Pound, P. G. Wodehouse). But for a hard-liner almost all American cinema must be accounted as reactionary, with a few of its greatest directors — Griffith, Ford, Vidor, Capra, Fuller — flagrantly so.

John Wayne up to his waist in direction – ***'GREEN BERETS'***

What is so repugnant about *The Green Berets* is not its politics (nor even, politics apart, its total ineptitude purely as an adventure war movie) but the fact that — in spite of overwhelming evidence to the contrary, evidence that by the late 60s had already filtered through to the United States — its makers were determined to reduce Vietnam to simple-minded Manichean antitheses: good guys versus bad guys, cowboys versus Indians, white men versus 'natives'. As Michael Wayne, the film's producer and its star's son, blandly put it to an interviewer from *Variety,* "Maybe we shouldn't have destroyed all those Indians, but when you are making a picture, the Indians are the bad guys." Why,

Green Berets colonel outlines Vietnamese action for skeptical war correspondent (David Janssen).

naturally. No-one – least of all, those who work there – expects Hollywood to learn a lesson from the past. And the myths and codes of popular fiction exert a powerful hold on the imagination, even if the intellect struggles to expulse them: many a movie buff with irreproachable opinions on race nevertheless continues to harbor a secret preference for the stereotypical black servants and Pullman car attendants of 30s screwball comedies — i.e. when Blacks 'knew their place' — over their emancipation in the 60s into aggressive leading roles. But the offense of Wayne and Son proved a dual one: not only did their movie provide a tritely simplified, almost *nostalgic* reading of what was in reality shot through with self-recriminations and self-exonerations, prejudice and sheer bad faith, but they attempted to impose such a reading while the war was still going on.

Consider, in *The Green Berets,* an atrocity tale recounted by the tough-named Colonel Mike Kirby (John Wayne). A journalist from what we gather is a liberal newspaper, George Beckworth (David Janssen), has flown out to Vietnam to 'see for himself' after being chided by Kirby at a press conference for judging events from a comfortable position of Stateside semi-ignorance. ("Hard to talk to anyone about this country until they've been over and seen it.") A myriad of little things like bamboo traps have chipped away at the rigor of Beckworth's antiwar stand (that he is in the movie at all has, of course, nothing to do with objectivity and everything to do with eventual conversion), but the incident that clinches matters involves, as always, a child. Beckworth had befriended the granddaughter of a Montagnard village headman and presented her with a medallion. Later, with Kirby, he visits the village to discover that the headman has been murdered by the Viet Cong and the little girl raped (or rather, in the movie's coy patois, 'abused') by five of them. As if this gangbang were not sufficiently horrible, Kirby immediately switches to hard sell by describing in gory detail to the shattered Beckworth a similar incident when a chieftain's wife was 'abused' by no fewer than *forty VC.* Here we are again in the shadowy area of logistics, though the basic problem is the reverse of *Holocaust*'s: not how do you *film* an atrocity, but how do you *invent* one. Why, for example, forty? Was thirty considered too few? A tentatively suggested sixty laughed out of the writers' room? Was the figure arrived at in proportion of horror to the little girl's five, as one year in a dog's life is reckoned to be comparable to a human's seven? Or did the calculation proceed along the lines of an auction, with bids steadily rising until forty was settled on as a nice round figure, not so high as to become preposterous but high enough to justify a liberal's conversion to the cause? Although the My Lai revelations were still to come, one is almost tempted to believe that the ante was upped so that American rapine — in the unlikely event of its existing at all — would be vindicated in advance by the comparison.

In a way, of course, this ploy would mirror the whole course of the war — viewed from the American side — toward *escalation,* as the inflation of interests led inexorably to a corresponding inflation of bloodshed. Even if the movie never encumbers its cliché-ridden narrative with so much as an atom of skepticism (except as far as Beckworth is concerned), its pathetic endeavors to contain an event as complex as Vietnam within genre structures that once seemed indestructible has lent it a kind of documentary value — and, incidentally, made it more watchable today than in 1968. One of the American cinema's strengths has

Pathos in the shape of the orphaned Hamchunk (Craig Jue). Journalist (David Janssen) begins to see the light.

always been its ability to disarm direct ideological criticism of a character's more dubious motives and actions by the behavioral charm of the performer portraying him or her (but mostly him). With its comic-relief 'scrounger' (Jim Hutton), hardboiled NCO (Aldo Ray), glamorous Oriental spy (Irene Tsu), sensitive black (Raymond St. Jacques) and overpoweringly cute local orphan (weren't any brats ever orphaned?), *The Green Berets* evidently hoped to make the old magic work for it, too. But something has gone seriously awry. Take Sgt. Provo (played by the aptly named Luke Askew). Early in the film, before the unit is shipped out to Vietnam, Provo volunteers for front-line duty as "I'd like to get orientated to the critical area." (As we'll see, the English language is made quite a meal of by everyone in this movie). Since Kirby is advised by an aide that Provo is a good soldier, he is duly assigned and, not unexpectedly, dies a hero's death. Now it's well nigh impossible to watch *The Green Berets* free of bias, but a critic especially must strive to keep an open mind. However, while viewing the movie it's difficult not to believe that the zombie-like

"...Maybe we shouldn't have destroyed all those Indians".

Provo, with his shorn head, granite features and robotized speech patterns, was being played as a psychopath or, at the very least, a severely disturbed war lover; that, in the context, he was the token representative (as Beckworth of liberalism) of a marginal but, alas, inescapable element of militarism and would receive his comeuppance in combat. Not at all: he is intended to be taken at face value, even offering with his death the choicest example of the movie's elephantine forays into humor. Provo is obsessively concerned with how his name would sound on a memorial. "Provo's Barracks, Provo's Commissary. Ya see what I mean — it just don't sing." As he lies dying, he whispers a last request to Kirby, who commissions a sign that reads "Provo's Privy", declaring gruffly, "It sings."

In a World War II movie this might conceivably have worked, minus the final gag. With William Bendix or Jack Carson as Provo, however implausible or antipathetic the character's eagerness to get to the front, one would probably have accepted it as a genre convention. Here, as with the Bilko-like scrounger Peterson, whose casual looting around the base is uneasily reminiscent of larger-scale corruption in South Vietnam, the stereotype has ceased to function. And when the orphan Hamchunk first endears himself to the audience by sending Peterson sprawling over a trip wire, we also have the uncomfortable (and no doubt unintended) impression that he will naturally graduate to playing with just the kind of bamboo trap that skewers Petersen in the end.

With its star, however, the gap between intention and realization widens as to become virtually unbridgeable. Unlike Bogart, whose brand of cynical idealism made him the (posthumous) idol of a whole generation of students and middle-class youth, Wayne was a blue-collar hero, the defender of traditional American values and sworn enemy of intellectuals, Communists and — what amounted to the same thing — perverts; particularly during the turbulent 60s and 70s, his appeal to educated young people tended to atrophy the moment they enrolled in college. This disaffection was nevertheless tempered by regular TV exposure to a career that could be considered distinguished by any standards (numerous films by Ford, Hawks, Wellman and Walsh) and by a grudging respect for the mythic figure he seemed to cut with such easy masculine grace and good humor. Many of the student radicals who despised Wayne's politics, his reprehensible cronies (Reagan, Agnew) and his deplorable public pronouncements (in a Playboy interview: "I've directed two pictures and I gave the blacks their proper position. I had a black slave in *The Alamo,* and I had the correct number of blacks in *The Green Berets")* retained a sneaking affection for the guts 'n' glory movies on which they had been weaned, so to speak, which had comprised the staple Saturday matinee fare in the neighborhood fleapits of their childhood, with the white screen serving as a kind of security blanket. Rare was the spectator capable of distinguishing actor from role and who, armed with this distinction — which in the latter, overtly ideological stage of Wayne's career was to become an increasingly fine one — could lace his enjoyment with irony, smugly keeping his distance from some more artless fan beside him. (Sadly, the elevation of Wayne to the status of national myth — consecrated by an Oscar in 1969 for his performance in Henry Hathaway's Western *True Grit* — came at the end of his life when a series of tiresome tic-ridden characterizations, all crust and no bread, had contrived to obscure his very real abilities).

That his movie alienated these smart-alecky college kids once and for all was surely of no consequence to Wayne; but even among his more unconditional admirers a certain embarrassment was felt. Since he had never bothered to keep his political sympathies to himself, it came as no surprise that *The Green Berets* turned out so rabidly pro-American. It was the very folly of his making a Vietnam movie in the first place that was hard to forgive, as if he had really believed in all those frontiersman myths about the taming of the Old West, as if he had never once stopped to wonder — with the offhand shrug of his son — whether "maybe we shouldn't have destroyed all those Indians". The Indians, it seems, were still to be typecast as the bad guys.

Nor were Wayne and screenwriter James Lee Barrett — the movie was based on a novel of the same name by Robin Moore — exactly subtle in the way they went about forging a link between Monument Valley (an Arizona beauty spot at which, before John Ford's camera crew arrived, no particularly memorable event in American history had occurred) and the jungles of South Vietnam. The movie's credit titles unroll to the accompaniment of a would-be stirring march tune "The Brave Men of the Green Beret"; over the entrance to a Special Forces outpost is a wooden ranch-style signpost reading "Dodge City"; when he and his men are forced to evacuate the camp after prolonged (and seemingly successful) attacks by the Vietcong, Kirby simply radios for an air strike, which arrives *à la* 1st Cavalry to polish off the intruders in a matter of minutes. There is Kirby's almost too familiar line "out here, due process is a bullet"; and the last scene is intended to be a quietly heart-tugging exchange at sunset between Kirby and Hamchunk, now doubly orphaned after the death of his mentor, Petersen, and obviously doomed to become regimental mascot. What makes these narrative trappings lodge so securely in the gullet is in part the movie's unerring awfulness; but if Ford, say, had directed it (not an impossible hypothesis, unfortunately), the result might have been even more revolting.

The Green Berets, however, is too inept to be effective, let alone dangerous. It's the film of an old, old man; and the sight of a sexagenarian John Wayne cavorting about the undergrowth in made-to-measure battle fatigues is not one calculated to strike terror in the hearts of the enemy — *or* the antiwar movement. All the flaws of his aging physique are cruelly exposed by what would appear to be a pitiful attempt to recapture his youth: the rolling hips, the enormous, top-heavy frame precariously perched on small, remarkably dainty feet, the craggy, weather-beaten features topped by an implausible toupee. Age and costume apart, the role could have been patched together from a montage of his past appearances, so derivative is every last gesture; every drawling syllable, every quizzical arch of the eyebrow. There is something slightly indecent in his thus personifying so barefacedly the schism of generations that was one of the war's most durable legacies: an old man playing a young man's game, one which many young men were no longer prepared to play. And one is struck by the fact that, except for the just middle-aged Jim Hutton (a refugee from 60s beach party movies), he is surrounded by actors hardly less ancient than himself: as Kirby's superior, the bloated Bruce Cabot (who once — a long time ago — rescued Fay Wray from the extrovert embrace of King Kong); and bull-faced Aldo Ray as one Sgt. Muldoon (ah Muldoon! a name to conjure with — no cavalry picture was ever without its truculent, rambunctious Muldoon, invariably hammed up by Victor MacLaglan). As for the 'correct number' of blacks, that would seem to be two, on the evidence of the speaking parts at least: Raymond St. Jacques, the soulful embodiment of Uncle Tomism (or Uncle Samism) and, in an unmemorable cameo, future stand-up comic Richard Pryor.

To be sure, one shouldn't forget the representative of youthful

"Out here, due process is a bullet" - Viet Cong prisoner in a tight spot.

unrest, David Janssen. In 1968 Janssen was thirty-eight, an age when the opinions of crusading journalists tend to be fully formed and impervious to the kind of abrupt ideological conversion that Beckworth undergoes in the movie. His radical chic finds a none too subtle sartorial equivalence in the Jungle Jim safari outfit he sports on arrival in Vietnam, just as his change of heart is expressed through a corresponding change of costume: he is soon in regulation fatigues. Having served his purpose by showing up the protest movement as founded on sheer blinkered ignorance (a premise contradicted by the testimony of numerous vets who returned from 'over there' only strengthened in their conviction that the American presence was both useless and criminal), he is more or less dispensed with by the narrative, which settles down to do its own war movie thing.

However, in view of the sluggishly routine combat sequences (which aren't — but look like — stock shots) and preposterous plot thickenings with the aforementioned glamorous spy (which, wherever one's sympathies lie, have absolutely *nothing* to do with any reality of the war), much the most interesting battle being waged is that against the forces of skepticism, as represented by Beckworth. Since, in lieu of a clear statement of eventual victory, *The Green Berets* concludes with no more than Kirby's piously phrased claim that South Vietnam would one day triumph over the Communist threat, it's all the more imperative that a victory — even if 'only' a moral one — be recorded against the peaceniks. The Green Berets, at the center of both conflicts, must therefore

Sgt. Peterson (Jim Hutton) falls foul of a Viet Cong booby trap.

Provo, with his shorn head, granite features and robotized speech patterns, was being played as a psychopath or, at the very least, a severely disturbed war lover; that, in the context, he was the token representative (as Beckworth of liberalism) of a marginal but, alas, inescapable element of militarism and would receive his comeuppance in combat. Not at all: he is intended to be taken at face value, even offering with his death the choicest example of the movie's elephantine forays into humor. Provo is obsessively concerned with how his name would sound on a memorial. "Provo's Barracks, Provo's Commissary. Ya see what I mean — it just don't sing." As he lies dying, he whispers a last request to Kirby, who commissions a sign that reads "Provo's Privy", declaring gruffly, "It sings."

In a World War II movie this might conceivably have worked, minus the final gag. With William Bendix or Jack Carson as Provo, however implausible or antipathetic the character's eagerness to get to the front, one would probably have accepted it as a genre convention. Here, as with the Bilko-like scrounger Peterson, whose casual looting around the base is uneasily reminiscent of larger-scale corruption in South Vietnam, the stereotype has ceased to function. And when the orphan Hamchunk first endears himself to the audience by sending Peterson sprawling over a trip wire, we also have the uncomfortable (and no doubt unintended) impression that he will naturally graduate to playing with just the kind of bamboo trap that skewers Petersen in the end.

With its star, however, the gap between intention and realization widens as to become virtually unbridgeable. Unlike Bogart, whose brand of cynical idealism made him the (posthumous) idol of a whole generation of students and middle-class youth, Wayne was a blue-collar hero, the defender of traditional American values and sworn enemy of intellectuals, Communists and — what amounted to the same thing — perverts; particularly during the turbulent 60s and 70s, his appeal to educated young people tended to atrophy the moment they enrolled in college. This disaffection was nevertheless tempered by regular TV exposure to a career that could be considered distinguished by any standards (numerous films by Ford, Hawks, Wellman and Walsh) and by a grudging respect for the mythic figure he seemed to cut with such easy masculine grace and good humor. Many of the student radicals who despised Wayne's politics, his reprehensible cronies (Reagan, Agnew) and his deplorable public pronouncements (in a Playboy interview: "I've directed two pictures and I gave the blacks their proper position. I had a black slave in *The Alamo,* and I had the correct number of blacks in *The Green Berets")* retained a sneaking affection for the guts 'n' glory movies on which they had been weaned, so to speak, which had comprised the staple Saturday matinee fare in the neighborhood fleapits of their childhood, with the white screen serving as a kind of security blanket. Rare was the spectator capable of distinguishing actor from role and who, armed with this distinction — which in the latter, overtly ideological stage of Wayne's career was to become an increasingly fine one — could lace his enjoyment with irony, smugly keeping his distance from some more artless fan beside him. (Sadly, the elevation of Wayne to the status of national myth — consecrated by an Oscar in 1969 for his performance in Henry Hathaway's Western *True Grit* — came at the end of his life when a series of tiresome tic-ridden characterizations, all crust and no bread, had contrived to obscure his very real abilities).

That his movie alienated these smart-alecky college kids once and for all was surely of no consequence to Wayne; but even among his more unconditional admirers a certain embarrassment was felt. Since he had never bothered to keep his political sympathies to himself, it came as no surprise that *The Green Berets* turned out so rabidly pro-American. It was the very folly of his making a Vietnam movie in the first place that was hard to forgive, as if he had really believed in all those frontiersman myths about the taming of the Old West, as if he had never once stopped to wonder — with the offhand shrug of his son — whether "maybe we shouldn't have destroyed all those Indians". The Indians, it seems, were still to be typecast as the bad guys.

Nor were Wayne and screenwriter James Lee Barrett — the movie was based on a novel of the same name by Robin Moore — exactly subtle in the way they went about forging a link between Monument Valley (an Arizona beauty spot at which, before John Ford's camera crew arrived, no particularly memorable event in American history had occurred) and the jungles of South Vietnam. The movie's credit titles unroll to the accompaniment of a would-be stirring march tune "The Brave Men of the Green Beret"; over the entrance to a Special Forces outpost is a wooden ranch-style signpost reading "Dodge City"; when he and his men are forced to evacuate the camp after prolonged (and seemingly successful) attacks by the Vietcong, Kirby simply radios for an air strike, which arrives *à la* 1st Cavalry to polish off the intruders in a matter of minutes. There is Kirby's almost too familiar line "out here, due process is a bullet"; and the last scene is intended to be a quietly heart-tugging exchange at sunset between Kirby and Hamchunk, now doubly orphaned after the death of his mentor, Petersen, and obviously doomed to become regimental mascot. What makes these narrative trappings lodge so securely in the gullet is in part the movie's unerring awfulness; but if Ford, say, had directed it (not an impossible hypothesis, unfortunately), the result might have been even more revolting.

The Green Berets, however, is too inept to be effective, let alone dangerous. It's the film of an old, old man; and the sight of a sexagenarian John Wayne cavorting about the undergrowth in prove themselves as nifty with words as with mere weapons. When conversing among each other, they employ a macho army rhetoric so elementary as to become almost self-parodic. E.g. ARVN colonel to Kirby: "We build many camps, clobber many VC. Affirmative?" Kirby: "Affirmative." And he adds: "I like the way you talk." *I like the way you talk.* Here's cultural imperialism with a vengeance. It's normal, one supposes, for the South Vietnamese to speak in English; in both a military and an exclusively cinematic context, it would raise awkward problems of communication if they didn't. But the infantile slang of 'clobber' and hideous militarese of 'affirmative'? Did the ARVN really talk like that? Are we really supposed to like it? Affirmative, or so it would appear.

When handling civilians and heretics, however, these same roughneck servicemen are transformed into smooth, even glib debaters, well-versed in dialectics and oozing quiet, long-suffering dignity from every pore. The movie opens in the USA at the John F. Kennedy Center (it sings!) for Special Warfare, Fort Bragg, North Carolina. A public demonstration of the training and qualities required of the Special Forces is in progress. The first words we hear are disconcertingly spoken in German; a unit leader, identifying himself and his mission, displays this apparently irrelevant gift for European languages to emphasize the truly international role played by the Green Berets (or maybe just in the hope of distracting his listeners' attention from more tropical and topical parts of the globe). When a number of these leaders have presented themselves in the same fashion (one of them bizarrely, if all too justifably, boasting a working knowledge of *English),* a question period follows, emceed by Sgt. Muldoon. The first question comes from a reporter seated in the front row and it's a biggie: "Why is the United States waging this useless war?" But Muldoon, a hard man to faze , is not about to give away any secrets: "A soldier goes where he is told to go, fights where he is told to fight." Touché.

Soon questions of the same type follow thick and fast, with no-one any longer terribly interested in the Green Berets' proficiency in German or Norwegian. Beckworth to McGee (Raymond St. Jacques): "Do you agree with that, Sgt. McGee? That the Green Beret is just a military robot with no personal feelings?" Muldoon seethes in the background. But Beckworth has made a serious tactical error in his choice of interlocutor: McGee has 'personal feelings' practically tattooed on his forehead. "Let me put it in terms we can all understand... If this same thing happened in the United States, every mayor in every city would be murdered. Every teacher... every professor... every Senator... every member of the House of Representatives..." (get on with it, man!) "... and their families... But in spite of this, there's always some little fellow out there willing to stand up and take the place of those who've been decimated. They need us... and they want us."

Fiendish Viet Cong looters at Fort Dodge.

Housewife: "It's strange that we never read of this in the newspapers."

Muldoon: "Well, that's newspapers for you, ma'am — you could fill volumes with what you *don't* read in them." Laughter, even from the press in the front row.

Beckworth, somewhat miffed that all the witty repartee seems to be coming from the other side: "That's sometimes very true, Sergeant. But how do you know we should be fighting for this present government? They've had no free elections. They have no constitution. Six months ago, a committee was appointed to form a constitution — still no constitution."

Whereupon Beckworth, the audience and the camera focus on Muldoon, who is rapidly shaping into *the* spokesman on American foreign policy. He clears his throat. "The school I went to taught us that the thirteen colonies, with proper and educated leadership, all with the same goal in mind, after the Revolutionary War, took from 1776 to 1787, eleven years of peaceful effort, before they came up with a paper that all thirteen colonies could sign." Pause. "Our present Constitution."

It's easy — not to say, child's play — to mock the crude didacticism of this scene, which is really in no need of ironic editorial comment. But since later Vietnam movies — in particular, Michael Cimino's *The Deer Hunter* (1979) — will use the same basic arguments, though cloaking them in a calculated and hypocritical ambiguity, it might be useful to examine the mechanism at its most rudimentary.

Clearly, the makers of *The Green Berets* saw McGee's "Let me put it in terms we can all understand" as their own primary task. This was to be no ordinary war movie. It had a *message.* But, with hindsight, McGee's phrase has unwittingly acquired an emblematic value: American involvement in Vietnam can be reduced to "terms we all understand" only if we adopt the ignorant, culture-bound view of history that was its root cause in the first place. After all, traditional Westerns may fairly claim to have put nineteenth-century American history in a perspective that everyone — even infants — can 'understand'. The Warners gangster movie cycle, albeit with greater equivocation, put the period of Depression and prohibition in terms that everyone could thrill to. Hollywood has always traded in the most artless kind of myths, consistently managing to palm them off on the same intelligent paying customers who would scorn such shoddy wares if offered them in literature or the theater. Its advantage (one it has never been reluctant to exploit) is that the myth-makers are generally at work before the historians. When the fullest implications of an event have finally begun to sink into the national consciousness (as with the Indian wars), there is already an established canon of much-loved movies whose very manipulation of historical accuracy is excused as having contributed an extra layer of sociological significance.

What changed with Vietnam is that, for the first time since the Civil War (a subject treated by Hollywood with surprising sensitivity), the nation found itself denied the reassurance of a broad consensus of opinion: decisions of urgent matter were openly, violently contested — in the streets, on campus — as they were being taken; history, as never before, was revised as it was being made. *The Green Berets* attempts to mythologize its heroes — the credit titles ballad, 'Big' Mike Kirby, the final sunset — but the myths are stillborn.

The movie's overall drift is patent, of course, but in that first sequence a number of precise points are being made, as an 'action replay' will demonstrate:

(1) The Green Berets never query or reflect upon the orders they receive: a soldier's job is to obey. In a period of even limited war, there can therefore be no excuse for draft dodgers or deserters.

(2) They are not, however, insensitive to human suffering, particularly where 'little fellows' are involved. The Viet Cong, buttressed by the vast ideological and military machine of world Communism (and the scene ends with Muldoon producing a cache of captured enemy armaments — of Chinese, Russian and East European provenance — presumably amassed for just such an occasion), do not qualify as 'little fellows'.

(3) Given this evidence of massive material aid from the whole Communist bloc, the apparent imbalance of forces engaged in the war is deceptive: what the United States is really up against is nothing less than, as Muldoon puts it, "Communist domination of the world".

(4) It *is* America's business to be in South-East Asia, since the inhabitants "need us and want us".

(5) If, however, the tribulations of a small, insignificant country thousands of miles away leave one uncaring, one should try to imagine a similar Communist insurrection within the United States, with the systematic liquidation of city mayors, teachers, etc. (A ludicrous analogy, invalidated by countless historical and geographical inequalities between the two countries, but one calculated to bring the war home, in both senses.)

(6) Don't believe everything you read in the newspapers.

(7) To Beckworth's reasonable objection that the brutal Thieu regime might not, after all, prove the lesser of two evils, Muldoon offers the eccentric but attractive theory that South Vietnam is fighting for the same freedoms as the founding colonies in 1776 and that any delay in the country's democratization only confirms its government's seriousness of purpose.

(8) With American aid, South Vietnam will surely prevail.

There, in a nutshell, are the pro-war lobby's main articles of faith, as propounded by numerous political and military executives, Washington columnists and a significant portion of the electorate. A few random quotes will suffice as illustration:

General Curtis LeMay (quoted in David Halberstam's *The Best and the Brightest*): "In the last thirty years we've lost Estonia. Latvia. Lithuania. Poland. Czechoslovakia. Hungary. Bulgaria. China..."

Cardinal Spellman in 1966: "This war in Vietnam, I believe, is a war for civilization... American troops are there for the defense, protection and salvation not only of our country, but I believe of civilization itself."

Vice President Agnew in 1972: The Vietnam war "is perhaps the most moral act the United States ever performed".

David Lawrence, editor of *U.S. News and World Report,* in 1966: "What the United States is doing in Vietnam is the most significant example of philanthropy... that we have witnessed in our times."

Future Presidential candidate Edward Kennedy in 1965: "We have a commitment in South Vietnam" and we "have to stand by our commitment".

Senator Strom Thurmond in 1968: "If we lose in Vietnam, before you know it the Communists would be up on the beaches of Hawaii."

A Saigon nightspot. . .

Major General Moshe Dayan of Israel in 1966: "The American army as a whole... gets satisfaction out of every day it spends in Vietnam... Most soldiers would volunteer for service in Vietnam if they were not posted there."

Senator Thomas Dodd in 1967: "If the Administration were to negotiate a settlement that paved the way for an early Communist take-over, then it will mark the total eclipse of America as a great nation and the beginning of the end of the entire free world."

To do justice to the wilful ignorance that characterized most pronouncements as to the war's outcome made by the political and military Establishment during these dark years, however, would need a chapter of its own, and what follows is only a modest sampling:

Political columnist Joseph Alsop in 1961: "The good guys have been coming out on top for once."

Secretary of Defense Robert McNamara in 1965: "We have stopped losing the war."

Vice President Hubert Humphrey in 1966: "There can be no doubt of our ultimate success."

General Maxwell Taylor in 1966: "The Viet Cong will just peter out."

Admiral John S. McCoin, Jr., Commander in Chief, Pacific, in

1969: "The enemy is beaten."

And political columnist Joseph Alsop once again in 1970: "Victory has at last been won."

As for the accusation often leveled against a partisan press that it deliberately misled its readers, though naturally not given much coverage in print, it was very much part of the received wisdom of the period. But it should be remembered that, long before the 'experts' began to temper their optimism (a cautious Gerald Ford in 1972: "Time is on our side"), a good many ordinary citizens had come to doubt the value and necessity of prolonging American involvement in South-East Asia.

The movie's opening sequence is therefore not only a rather wordy piece of exposition to introduce the Beckworth character but an example of virtually undiluted propaganda (of a type rare in the American cinema), and an indirect measure of how important it was considered for the domestic market is the fact that it was cut from several European prints. Worth noting, too, is that *The Green Berets* is still the *only* Hollywood movie to have tackled the issues of the war head on (even if with heavily loaded arguments) and from an ideological standpoint that it endorses without flinching (even if its anticommunism is of the Pavlovian variety). The few films to have focused on Vietnam from the antiwar angle and whose political discourse is not risibly subservient to the same old apolitical priorities of heroism (for our boys) and human dignity (for the friendly natives) have either

But Vietnam wasn't all fun . . . Col. Mike Kirby, Lin (Irene Tsu) and Col. Cai, (Jack Soo)

been documentaries (e.g. Emile De Antonio's *In the Year of the Pig,* 1969 and Peter Davis' *Hearts and Minds,* 1974) or non-American (e.g. the French compendium film *Loin du Viêtnam,* 1967).

After losing game, set and match to the army, Beckworth approaches Kirby who — perhaps in deference to Muldoon — had stood on the sidelines throughout the preceding debate.

Beckworth: "Colonel, your brainwashed sergeant didn't sell me."

Kirby: "Didn't sell you what?"

Beckworth: "Didn't sell me on the idea that we should be in South-East Asia."

Kirby: "You ever been to South-East Asia?"

Beckworth: "No, I haven't."

Kirby: "Huh!"

At which point the film, like Beckworth himself, visibly intrigued by that cathartic "huh!", shifts to the combat zone (and the second unit to the state of Georgia for location shooting). As Petersen, screaming above the roar of the helicopter taking him into the Vietnamese hinterland, hopefully puts it: "With joyous memories we leave the mystical city of Da Nang. What gay adventures lie ahead? Brother, this trip is gonna make LSD feel like aspirin."

Wrong. It makes aspirin feel like LSD. For all that the movie's premise is that Vietnam the war can only be judged by someone who has been to Vietnam the country, its portrait of local conditions is geared to confirm the worst prejudices of Middle American homebodies. Although screenwriter Barrett himself flew out to South Vietnam for the purposes of research (and, according to Dan Wakefield's *Supernation at Peace and War,* among the many things that impressed him over there was the attitude expressed by one officer who told him that "These people don't want to be free, but by God, we're going to *make* them free!" "To me," Barrett said, "that's a new and exciting concept."), the cursory and implausible results suggest he might just as well have stayed in Beverly Hills watching old World War II and Korean war movies on TV. The Viet Cong are depicted as a confused horde of whirling dervishes, milling around the Green Beret strike camp to minimal effect; the only one to stand out in a crowd is a high-ranking General, a corrupt tyrant who lives it up in a luxuriously appointed French colonial villa guarded by uniformed thugs. The South Vietnamese, however, are a different race entirely: dogged allies displaying a faith in American goodwill so unswerving that one would have to go back to the Liberation of Paris in 1944 to find its equal.

The only example of Vietnamese culture we are permitted to see (and whose 'defense, protection and salvation' is supposedly the Green Berets' *raison d'être)* is an El Cheapo nightclub in Da

Off-camera glamor pose for carefully smudged Irene Tsu and John Wayne.

Nang which Kirby visits in company with his local counterpart, Colonel Cai. Its floor show consists of a maudlin Parisian ballad sung by a young woman in a shantung slit skirt; and at a nearby table sits Lin, the Vietnamese Mata Hari ("Besides being one of our country's top models, she could be most useful to the government"). Subsequently, Lin will deploy her top model's charms as bait, in a raid led jointly by Kirby and Cai, to kidnap the VC general, a sequence which, though tediously predictable in its plotting, does shed a brief light on the nation's overly developed sense of morality. Lin is obliged to sleep with the general, a sacrifice (especially in view of the fact that her father was murdered by the Viet Cong) which nevertheless causes her to be ostracized by Cai, who happens to be her cousin. It takes a moving little man-to-man speech from Kirby to persuade Cai to welcome her back into the family bosom.

On the American side, the movie is hardly less sketchy. No mention is made of napalm (except as a handy means of 'clearing' the jungle), body counts, body bags, free-fire zones, search-and-destroy missions, etc. The Green Berets, it is understood, fight by the Queensberry Rules, all the more commendably in the face of enemy methods as dastardly as bamboo booby-traps, which somehow come across as the ultimate in destructive weaponry. Although torture is used at one point in the interrogation of a VC fifth columnist, it is phlegmatically condoned by Kirby as a necessary evil to which, in any case, the Viet Cong are more than equal, as an outraged Beckworth is soon to discover for himself. Yet, in spite of its apparently non-committal but in fact wholeheartedly committed blandness vis-a-vis the horrors of this war, the movie cannot disguise the fact that a military (and cinematic) mythos is going sour before our eyes. I doubt if it is only liberals who are disturbed by the zeal with which Wayne at the "Dodge City" outpost calls on the air force to "move the jungle back" and provide him with "a clear killing zone"; or Aldo Ray's mischievous grin when, during the kidnap raid, he blows a bridge full of scurrying VC to kingdom come; or, in a different register, the poignant scene where Jim Hutton takes Hamchunk into his bed. And when, after the initial misfortune of being orphaned, Hamchunk loses first his puppy (from the same cute litter as the one in *Apocalypse Now)* then Petersen, it rather begins to look, as Lady Bracknell would say, "like carelessness".

Even if the turgid green and brown tonality of Winston Hoch's photography makes the whole movie seem to have been camouflaged, not once does one get a sense of the lived experience of soldiers at war. The squad is the usual ethnic cross-section, boasting such names as Muldoon, Provo, Petersen, 'Doc' McGee, Jamison (a young Lieutenant played by Wayne's son Patrick), MacDaniel and Kowalski. Notwithstanding Petersen's fleeting reference to LSD and ambiguous use of the word 'trip', there is no hint of the counter-culture orientation toward drugs, rock music and generalized subversion of authority that significantly changed the public image of the American army in the late 60s. But then, there was no need for the 'good guys' to change (unlike in *M*A*S*H**, made only two years later), as the enemy had so patently been preserved in amber, the swarthy amber complexion of all wily Orientals from Fu Manchu onward.

For anyone who has ever mused on what it must feel like for a German or Japanese spectator to be confronted with a Hollywood war movie, *The Green Berets* offers a close approximation. Viewed from hindsight, the morale-boosting optimism — tinged with melancholy for the fallen Provo and Petersen — with which it intends to leave us is disheartening beyond words: one is tempted to interpret the lurid sunset against which Kirby declares to his newest 'recruit', Hamchunk, that "You're what this war is all about" as the light at the end of the tunnel sinking definitively out of sight. There is, too, a final exchange between Kirby and Beckworth:

Kirby: "Whatya gonna say in that newspaper of yours?"
Beckworth: "If I say what I feel, I may be out of a job."
Kirby: "We'll always give you one."
Beckworth: "I could do you more good with a typewriter."

One can only speculate as to how the hapless Beckworth would fare in the 70s, a period when investigative journalism (thanks to such media superstars as Bernstein and Woodward, David Halberstam and the Washington muckraker Jack Anderson) was to become the most modish of professions.

In spite (perhaps because) of the widespread and also widely publicized picketing of theaters exhibiting *The Green Berets,* it proved a solid commercial success, grossing more than eight million dollars in domestic returns alone. However, one should avoid hasty conclusions. Since no direct causal link has ever been established between the political Zeitgeist and movie attendances, these figures probably tell us more about the popularity of John Wayne than about the breadth of public support for the war. So total, for example, was the identification of actor with role in Mark Rydell's *The Cowboys* (1971) that the film was distributed in France as *John Wayne et les cowboys* and, had *The Green Berets* not opened in the immediate aftermath of May '68, it could well have been retitled *John Wayne et les Berets Verts.* In short, it was very much Wayne's movie: as far as the industry was concerned, his involvement put Vietnam on the map (even as it blasted it off). Which perhaps explains why, in spite of those eight million dollars, no major studio was willing to undertake another movie set in Vietnam until well into the 70s.

But Wayne may after all have had an influence on the course of Hollywood's treatment of the war. There was a vast youthful audience out there just waiting to be tapped. And *The Green Berets had* succeeded in mobilizing that audience — if not to the point of bringing them into the theaters, at least in getting them to stand outside in protest...

SECTION III
SON OF VIETNAM

A SOCIAL historian whose data were entirely confined to film would be forgiven for surmising that young people — i.e. teenagers — constituted a relatively recent phenomenon, dating at most from the late 50s and early 60s. With rare exceptions, and though boasting every variety of child — including a handful (in both senses) of child stars — Hollywood's previous four decades paid astonishingly scant attention to a generation that must have been statistically almost as numerous as it is today. Even the exceptions were deceptive. When, in Busby Berkeley's MGM musical *Babes in Arms* (1939), a youthful Mickey Rooney and Judy Garland decide to put on a show *"right here* - in the barn!", they were both seventeen. But, apart from the fact that the title number "We're only babes in arms" is given a rather overpowering rendition by the kind of stocky baritone it is hard to imagine in any mother's arms, the very talent and exuberance of the performers, coupled with the innocence and enthusiasm of the characters they portray, were far too remote from all those agonizing, post-pubertal problems for any young moviegoer to identify with them.

Nothing could be further removed from their innocuous capers, however, than the unrelieved torments of 50s movie adolescents, who all appeared to have attended Method acting courses in high school; with Laslo Benedek's *The Wild One* (1953) and Nicholas Ray's *Rebel Without A Cause* (1955) the sleepyhead stumblebum charisma of Brando, Dean *et al* was unleashed on a startled world. Unlike Rooney and Garland, these young protagonists were intended for an equally young audience and not to indulge the older generation in wistful wish-fulfillment fantasies. Adolescence was depicted pimples and all, a second baptism in which the rocky road to manhood (girls were rarely more than 'girlfriends') abounded in such existential toll-gates as the automobile 'chicken run' in *Rebel Without A Cause* and the prostitute who, in Elia Kazan's *Splendor in the Grass* (1961), initiates Warren Beatty into the mysteries of carnal love.

These two strains, Rooney and Brando, converged to foster the explosion of movies for, about and on occasion by youth which marked the late 60s (often with the original iconography intact: the prototype Hell's Angels of *The Wild One* were adopted as consciously assumed models for *Easy Rider's* Peter Fonda and Dennis Hopper on their gleaming Harley Davidsons). The period also saw a relaxation of censorship, permitting themes of sex, drugs and radical politics to be more freely aired, without at the same time subjecting them to the traditional Hays Code catch that conformity invariably triumph in the final reel. The story has been told too often of how Hollywood, flushed with the mammoth box-office success of a few blockbuster musicals (most notably Robert Wise's *The Sound of Music* in 1965), embarked on a misbegotten cycle of hopefully similar projects (e.g. Richard Fleischer's *Doctor Dolittle,* 1967, Wise's *Star!,* 1968, and Gene Kelly's *Hello Dolly,* 1969) which cost as much and earned far less,

Billy (Dennis Hopper), Wyatt (Peter Fonda) and temporary passenger George Hanson (Jack Nicholson) take to the road – ***'EASY RIDER'***

Billy lies bleeding, having been gunned down by outraged locals in the same movie.

just as a relatively low-budget feature made by an untested actor-turned-director, Dennis Hopper's *Easy Rider* (1969), was raking in a fortune for its backers.

With the nonchalance of a tourist changing cable-cars in San Francisco, the major studios coolly proceeded to leap off one bandwagon visibly going nowhere fast onto another headed in the opposite direction. There followed a veritable rage (like 'wild', a very 60s word) for youth-oriented movies. If most of these, too, proved commercial disasters, it was perhaps because the very barrage of product denied them the 'sleeper' cult status that had made *Easy Rider* so beguiling to its audience, the sense of a generation long excluded from proportional representation in the American cinema discovering and appropriating the movie as 'one of ours'. Not only were the post-*Easy Rider* films much too aggressively angled at this new, moneyed section of the public,

Cool pool from leather-clad Peter Fonda. Michael J. Pollard stands in awe – ***'WILD ANGELS'***

there were too many writers, producers and directors involved whose sole affinity with the subject-matter — unlike Hopper's — was an opportunistic one.

This said, it has to be admitted that *Easy Rider* itself, though indisputably one of the key Zeitgeist movies of the 60s, is virtually unwatchable today. It tells of two young dropouts, Billy (Hopper) and Wyatt (Fonda), nicknamed 'Captain America', who sell a consignment of cocaine to a wealthy pusher near the Mexican border, stow the cash payment in Wyatt's fuel tank and set out across America on their custom-built motorcycles (the Harley Davidson came to symbolize the period as, say, the Hispano-Suiza automobile had done for the 20s), their only goal being to reach New Orleans in time for Mardi Gras. But their long hair, hippie garb and psychedelically painted machines cause them to be refused by motels and attacked by a lynching party; a commune in New Mexico where they spend some time comes to grief through its members' urban ignorance of basic manual and agricultural skills; their experiment with acid in a New Orleans cemetery turns into a horrendously bad trip; and they both meet violent deaths, gunned down almost 'for fun' by a passing truckdriver.

What *is* interesting about this See America First odyssey is that, for once, the movie's protagonists seem to derive as much sensual pleasure from the visual exploration of the landscapes they traverse (hauntingly if rather luridly shot by cinematographer Laszlo Kovaks) as, vicariously, does its audience. Seeing, of course, is a function of the kind of vision one possesses rather than of what there is in front of one; Hopper's direction, unfortunately, never articulates a coherent point of view. The bigoted redneck farmers, the lynching party, even the wan, weatherbeaten hippies have all been co-opted into embodying the moral bankruptcy of a country ready at the slightest provocation to explode into aggression and violence; but it remains mistily unclear where the two inarticulate, drug-pushing and eventually martyred heroes (filmed — especially blond, blue-eyed Fonda — as if candidates for counterculture canonization) stand in relation to the general malaise. Hanson, an alcoholic civil rights lawyer who secures their release from prison (played with his usual fiendish charm by Jack Nicholson), muses sadly: "You know, this used to be hell of a good country. I can't understand what's gone wrong with it." But the nostalgia which permeates the movie is totally unfocused: the country as it 'used to be' would no more gladly have tolerated these misfits who, in any case, are quite prepared to contribute to its potential for violence by dealing in hard drugs.

Easy Rider is fatally pinned between a facile (and premature) *fin de siecle* romanticism — Hopper's pet visual trope is letting the sun dazzle the camera lens — and an unrealized ambition to conjure the moment when the American Dream also turned into a 'bad trip'. Like some mobile sculpture, the glistening chrome surfaces of its heroes' motorcycles reflect only random fragments of contemporary disquiet; and, ultimately, the movie is undone by its own intrusive narcissism, as if, not content merely to contemplate his navel, Hopper had decided to film it in grainy close-up. What cruelly lacked was an objective factor that would concentrate the genuine disillusionment and direct it against a more substantial target than mere small town bigotry. Vietnam was to be that factor. To a 60s mythology that, even before the turning point of *Easy Rider,* had been exploited by such movies as *The Wild Angels* (1966), about a Nazi-inspired motorcycle gang, and *The Trip* (1967), about a controlled LSD experience, both directed by Roger Corman and starring Peter Fonda, was added the war. A war, however, that was cautiously conjugated in the past (returning vets) or future tense (anxieties over the draft).

Though the first of the specifically protest movement movies, in which the Rooney-Garland cry was updated to "Let's put on the war *right here* - on campus!", surfaced only one year later in 1970 (Stuart Hagmann's *The Strawberry Statement* and Richard Rush's *Getting Straight),* in some respects the richest works were those whose relation to the war was more oblique. The movement had its own dynamic, its own heroes and martyrs, even its own atrocities (e.g. the Kent State killings), so that the demonstrations of solidarity at home often appeared curiously unconnected with the antipodean war that prompted them. A case in point is Michelangelo Antonioni's *Zabriskie Point* (1969) almost universally panned as either a cynical exploitation of the youth market or as an ignorantly superficial response to the troubled vitality of America's contemporary landscape by an aging, patrician, European 'art movie' director. How could one take seriously, the argument ran, a movie that proceeds from the realistically edgy concourse of a group of radical militants (presided over by the formidable Mrs Eldridge Cleaver) to the cop-out apocalypse of its climax, when Daria (Daria Halprin) visualizes in her mind's eye the destruction — in slow motion, even — of her millionaire employer's opulent desert villa?

American critics doubtless expected an intellectual of Antonioni's stature to have 'something to say' about student revolutionaries and the deep divisiveness of opinion over the war (why? since his *Blow Up,* 1966, had said virtually nothing about Swinging London). But here campus unrest, almost autonomous of any larger political context, seems more fixated on the domestic guardians of the nation's foreign policy (the police) than on the import of that policy itself — at one point, after some

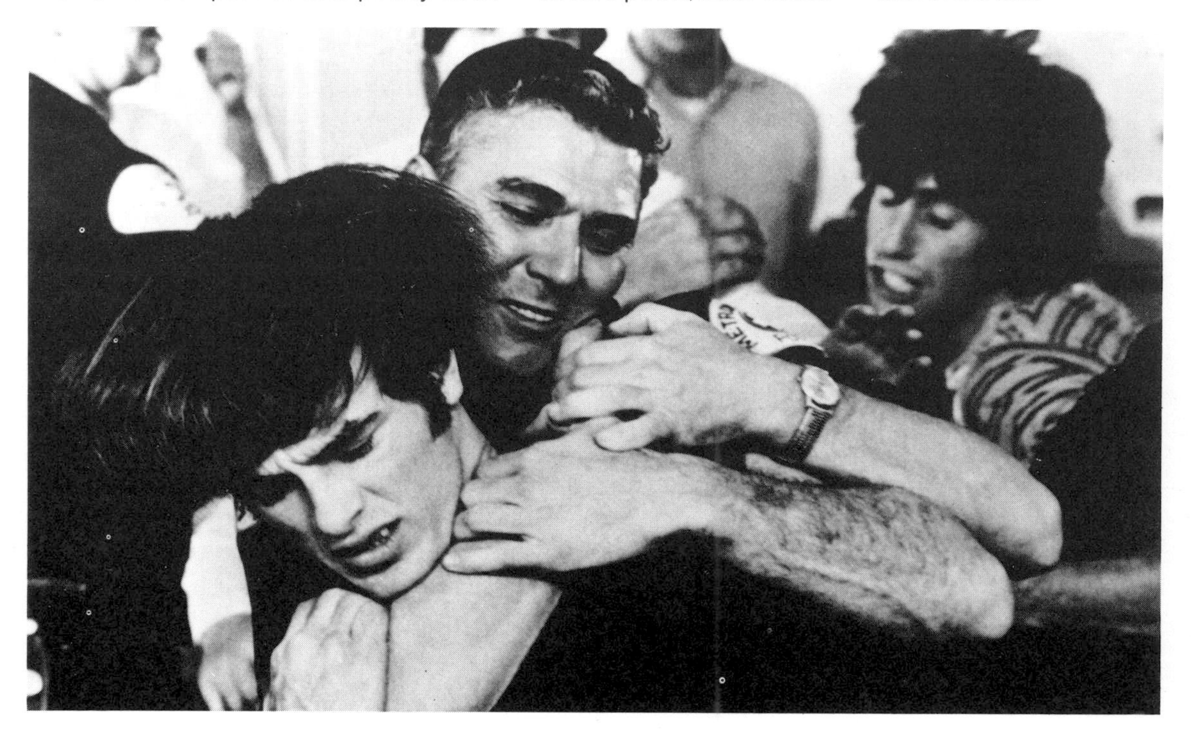

Mark (Mark Frechette) bound up by the strong arm of the law.

Psychedelic camouflage for Mark's airplane. Daria (Daria Halprin) admires the design — ***'ZABRISKIE POINT'***

arrests have been made, a Social Professor of History is contemptuously entered in police records as 'clerk'. As Antonioni sensed, the war — a pressing problem, to be sure, for those about to be drafted — more generally served at best to *centralize* a spirit of rebellion that was already, if diffusely, in the air; at worst to perpetuate and legitimize any confused, half-motivated violence. But he also saw, and expressed through poetic rather than analytical insights, the extent to which this disaffection was itself a child of the conspicuous capitalism that it professed to reject. For all their well-intentioned cant about 'alternative life-styles', these young people remain the fauna of America's surrealistically beautiful panorama — where the desert paradoxically offers an oasis from the smog-haloed city and, as in a Magritte painting, a breathtaking natural vista may be obscured by a huge billboard advertising just such a vista. Even in revolt, they are slavishly dependent on its most sophisticated artefacts: the private airplane stolen by Mark (played by an unknown, Mark Frechette, later to be killed in a prison brawl) no less than *Easy Rider's* Harley Davidsons stuffed with dollar bills. And the final explosive destruction is so stylized as to become a Creation in reverse, a magnificent firework display of America's material plenitude.

But the uncritical wonderment at this plenitude shared by most European diectors caused them to see both sides alike as part of the same affectionately or sourly observed set of phenomena. Jacques Demy's *The Model Shop* (1969), about the last mournful fling enjoyed by a young architect (Gary Lockwood) before his drafting, emerged as a bluesy hymn to the seedy, peeling labyrinth of downtown Los Angeles, the war itself being little more than an offscreen *deus ex machina. Taking Off* (1971) was a slight, droll, over-extended comedy of the generation gap, with both parents and children viewed as endearing freaks in the distorting mirror of director Milos Forman's somewhat mean-spirited brand of naturalism (an amateur rock contest entirely peopled by pasty complexioned teenage girls, a banquet sponsored by the 'Society for the Parents of Fugitive Children', during which assorted mothers and fathers make their first maladroit attempts at smoking marijuana, etc); and the war, one supposes, just out of earshot.

His slick, meretricious *One Flew Over the Cuckoo's Nest* (1975), by turning Ken Kesey's novel into a showcase for Jack Nicholson's irrepressible rapist intent on liberating (but only in the psychological sense) his fellow asylum inmates, neatly lobotomized the allegorical paranoia of the original. And it's typical of Forman's softie cynicism that when his work finally acknowledged the existence of a war behind all these hallucinatory high jinks, Vietnam had become, in *Hair* (1979), a suitable subject for nostalgia and Flower Power the 60s Art Déco.

Another indication of how cagily Hollywood broached the subject of the war is the fact that the closest Arthur Penn has ever got to it (at least, as I write this) is *Alice's Restaurant* (1969). Penn would seem to possess all the requisite credentials for making a solid contribution to Vietnam cinema: his espousal of liberal causes *(Little Big Man,* 1970), his sympathy for marginals of every hue *(The Left-Handed Gun,* 1958, *The Miracle Worker,* 1962, respectively about Billy the Kid and Helen Keller, and *Bonnie and Clyde,* 1967) and perhaps over-acute sensitivity to paranoia (the intolerably pretentious fable *Mickey One,* 1965, and tolerably pretentious *noir* thriller *Night Moves,* 1975). *Alice's Restaurant,* expanded from Arlo Guthrie's twenty-minute talking blues *The Alice's Restaurant Massacree,* is both the impressionistic celebration and bleakly detached post-mortem of a small community of misfits who run through a representative roster of 60s panaceas: drugs, music, communal living and the kind of all-

'The Generation Gap Closes' – parents try it for themselves in Milos Forman's ***'TAKING OFF'***

*Ex-vet R. P. McMurphy (Jack Nicholson) considers the other side of the wire – **'ONE FLEW OVER THE CUCKOO'S NEST'***

embracing love that should have a flower sticking out of its vase-like 'v'. All-embracing, however, in a rigorously unphysical sense, as Arlo firmly declines the advances of his benefactress Alice (Pat Quinn) just as, conversely, the truckdriver who has given him a lift rapidly cools toward him when he sees his long hair cascading from beneath a Stetson. As Tom Milne has written, Arlo's more famous father Woody, the Dustbowl balladeer, "spent his life going towards life rather than dropping out of it": vague, universally applicable 'love' all too frequently risks being unrequited.

Vietnam is twice woven into the movie's narrative. It first leads Arlo to Alice's deconsecrated church in Vermont (after being run out of a college in which he had enrolled to obtain draft deferment); and it's a Thanksgiving dinner at her restaurant that enables him to avoid military service (having helpfully dumped the Thanksgiving garbage, he is jailed as a litterbug and later

McMurphy flips and strikes an orderly, earning a course of electric shock treatment.

rejected at an induction center as an unrehabilitated criminal). Astonishingly but agreeably, both arresting officer and sentencing judge were played in the movie — well played, too — by the actual functionaries who inspired the *Massacree.*

Haskell Wexler's *Medium Cool* (1969) — the title refers to McLuhan's distinction of hot and cool media — is the study of a TV news cameraman's progressive radicalization in the late 60s. In parallel to the course of Wexler's own career from cinematographer of other directors' work (*In the Heat of the Night, Who's Afraid of Virginia Woolf?*) to director and scenarist of his own, it traces its protagonist's political education from his initially uncurious recording of news items ("Jesus! I love to shoot film!") to direct and even dangerous involvement in them, culminating in an extraordinary sequence in which the two parallels, so to speak, converge. John (Robert Forster) has been assigned to cover a tactical exercise at a National Guard riot training camp, where a group of folk-singing Guardsmen in plain clothes, i.e. hippie garb, confront their bayonet-bearing comrades in conventional uniform, tear gas explodes and, on the soundtrack, an alarmed voice is heard yelling to the director (who

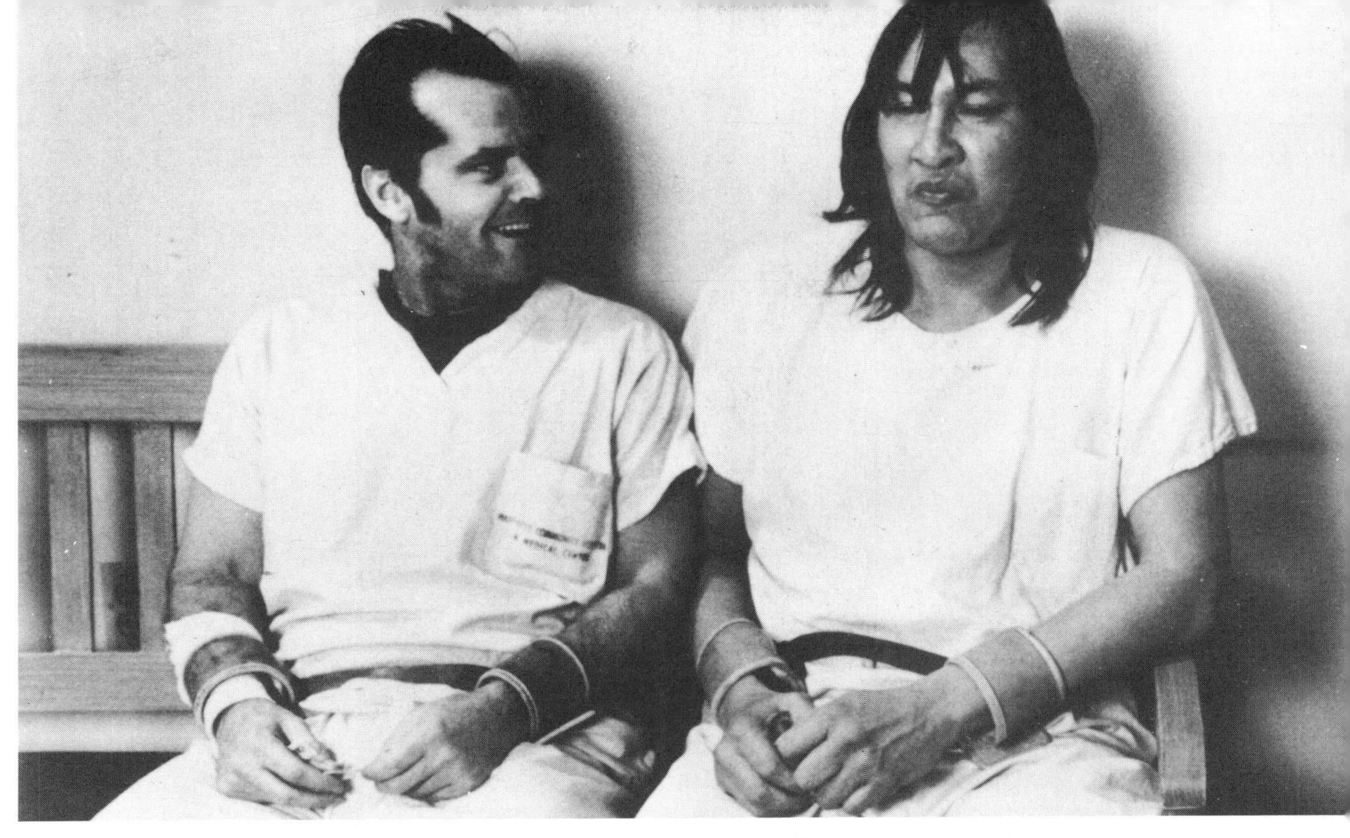

'Waiting for the electrode'. Chief Bromden (Will Sampson) speaks for the first time.

was in fact gassed while shooting the scene): "Look out, Haskell, it's real!" Unfortunately, much of this glossy 'photographer's film' is less authentic, from its facile visual rhymes clicking into place (the movie opens with John dispassionately filming an automobile accident while the mangled victim still groans for help and ends with his own crash, coolly snapped by a teenager from the back seat of a passing car) to its glib narrative strategies (one routine assignment coincidentally acquaints him with the existence of black militancy, another with the horrifying depths of poverty in the Appalachians). There is, however, some fascinating coverage of the turbulent 1968 Democratic Convention in Chicago and the brutally policed demonstrations surrounding it. Two other parallel lines meet here. John has discovered with indignation that the FBI and CIA have automatic access to his footage: ironically, Wexler's *own* twenty hours of Convention footage was subsequently requisitioned by the Justice Department.

Though the distribution of *Medium Cool* was handled by a major studio, Paramount, its tyro director, absence of stars and semi-documentary style bracket it rather with the 'new Hollywood', or with movies whose relation to the industry was either marginal or (in the case of Robert Kramer) nonexistent. In the 70s, the unlovely term 'movie brats' was coined for a generation of, by Hollywood's standards, extremely young directors whose childhoods seem to have been spent almost exclusively in movie theaters. Thus they were also described as 'cine-literate' (implying, however, a very narrow definition of literacy: the movies which they knew by heart, quoted from or pastiched in their own work are just the kind of popular 'classics'

Arlo Guthrie awaits his turn to face the draft board – ***'ALICE'S RESTAURANT'***

familiar to anyone with a reasonably developed interest in cinema). They lived and breathed movies, were animated by a passion for the medium that tended to override any lingering doubts as to whether they might have something significant to contribute to it.

As generally labeled, there are six of them: Francis Coppola, Brian De Palma, George Lucas, John Milius, Steven Spielberg and Martin Scorsese. To these might be added a scenarist who was eventually to graduate to the director's chair, Paul Shrader. Some of them were students at USC or UCLA, they regularly screened rough cuts of their movies for each other, their professional capacities frequently overlapped: Coppola helped finance Lucas's *American Graffiti,* Milius wrote the original script for *Apocalypse Now,* Lucas produced and co-scripted Spielberg's *Raiders of the Lost Ark,* etc. By dint of a few unparalleled box-office triumphs (*The Godfathers I and II,* 1972 and '74, *Jaws,* 1975, *Close Encounters of the Third Kind,* 1977, *Taxi Driver,* 1976, *American Graffiti* and *Star Wars,* 1977 — only Milius and De Palma, to their chagrin, have seen such monstrous success consistently elude them), these young Turks all managed prematurely to install themselves in positions of power within the Hollywood system. They acquired freedom. They could take risks (Scorsese's mammoth 'big band' musical, *New York, New York,* 1977, Spielberg's indigestible thirty million dollar slice of slapstick pie, *1941,* 1979, and, an especial risk for these inflationary times, Coppola's *normally* budgeted study of paranoia in the age of electronics, *The Conversation,* 1974). If they had been so inclined, they could certainly have raised financing for movies about the war. But while it would be self-righteously puritanical to censure them for failing to seize this opportunity of becoming the spokesmen of their contemporaries drafted to (and sometimes killed in) Vietnam, it can't be denied that their record on the matter is disappointing, to say the least.

From the two unrepentant entertainers, Spielberg and Lucas, hardly a whisper. Spielberg's dopey but diverting movies visibly aspire to the condition of the cartoon. His sole foray into war movie territory, the epically gross farce *1941,* focused on an invasion that did not even materialize: the unfounded rumors of further Japanese aggression which swept Southern California in the immediate aftermath of Pearl Harbor. But his regressive infantilism is more than matched by that of Lucas who, after an unsuccessful essay in Orwellian science-fiction — a movie that bore, in lieu of a title, a registration number *THX-1138* (thereby endorsing the common sci-fi assumption that such currently arcane letters of the alphabet as X and Z will in the future become quite run-of-the-mill) — settled for a career of unreflecting but highly marketable nostalgia. *American Graffiti* was a clever 'neon-realist' evocation of the sounds, attitudes and mannerisms of the Eisenhower era, a movable feast of junk food as its four young protagonists cruised through the garish streets of a small town in Northern California (pieced together from San Rafael, Petaluma and San Francisco) on the last night of their adolescence: an end title card spelling out their respective futures informed us that the unprepossessing Terry (Charlie Martin Smith), nicknamed 'the Toad' and the epitome of every kid's 'loser' friend, would be killed in combat in Vietnam. It's as much a tribute to the movie's uncanny 50s reconstruction as to its actors' behavioral charm that the death of one pimpled, bespectacled, good-natured adolescent could with such conviction encapsulate the end of an epoch.

At the same time, however, Lucas's calculated escapism, his wilful evasion of the divided period in which he was living for one

Joy of release from jail – ***'ALICE'S RESTAURANT'***

Campus unrest –
'MEDIUM COOL'

socially and politically so conformist were scarcely irrelevant to *American Graffiti's* unprecedented box-office returns (greater, proportionally to what it cost, than those of *Star Wars*). If the movie's motorized pyrotechnics recalled a dodgem car race (and should properly be viewed at a drive-in), *Star Wars* twitched and blinked across the Panavision screen like a gigantic pinball machine, a resemblance which, paradoxical as this may seem, contrived to set it even further into the past: less because it bore no relation to any of the planet's foreseeable futures (a given of science fiction) than in the systematic way it fed upon the mythical narrative archetypes — Westerns, Samurai films, medieval adventures, *The Wizard of Oz* and Road Runner cartoons — of childhood reading and moviegoing. In fact, it was just the kind of movie that would have played to packed houses in *American Graffiti's* boulevard Bijou.

Apart from writing a scenario for *Apocalypse Now,* Milius alluded to Vietnam in his own weird surfing saga, *Big Wednesday* (1978), notably in a farcical scene of draft induction. But once again the war — to which the most sympathetic and readily indentifiable of the three bronzed friends goes willingly — is treated, not as the death knell but the culminating point of 60s nostalgia. Though in some incidentals a striking movie (the use of a beach gateway, invariably filmed from the same angle, to frame the action like a classical portico in Greek tragedy), its faintly theological approach to the hermetic sport of surfing and ludicrous macho posturings limited its appeal to strictly local (i.e. Southern Californian) consumption.

Coppola's *Apocalypse Now,* the sole head-on confrontation of a movie brat with the war itself, and Scorsese's *Taxi Driver* will be treated in subsequent chapters. But one of the best of the 'draft' movies, incongruously from a director who now specializes in hysterical, crypto-Hitchcockian shockers, was Brian DePalma's

Twisting the night away at the High School dance – ***'AMERICAN GRAFFITI'***

Terry 'The Toad' (Charlie Martin Smith) and Debbie (Candy Clarke) cruising – ***'AMERICAN GRAFFITI'***

Yes, they are wearing bathing shorts. Matt (Jan-Michael Vincent), Leroy (Gary Busey) and Jack (William Katt) in search of the perfect wave.

Greetings (1968). DePalma's background was East Coast, and the miniscule budgets allotted to his first New York-based movies, *The Wedding Party* (1964) and *Murder a la Mod* (1968), did not extend to professional casts (though the former — retroactively, as it were — remains his starriest production to date: two of his friends who appeared in it were Jill Clayburgh and Robert De Niro). These juvenile efforts, as if in dual homage to moviemakers as dissimilar, even diametrically opposed, as Godard and Hitchcock, confusedly sought to challenge the spectator's perceptions and manipulate his emotions at the same time. As one might expect, there *were* few spectators.

But *Greetings,* brashly launched on a privately raised 10,000 dollars and finally budgeted at 43,000, brought in more than a million. The movie (whose title alludes to the deceptively genial first word read by recipients of US Army conscription papers) builds up a surprisingly rich mosaic of 60s fringe culture out of the off-beat obsessions of three New York dropouts during the two weeks that separate their draft medical examination from its results. Paul (Jonathan Warden) is preoccupied by a series of inconclusive computer-selected dates; Lloyd (Gerritt Graham), a Kennedy assassination addict, makes contact with a bizarre figure who claims to be the seventeenth and sole surviving witness to Oswald's movements following the crime; and Jon (De Niro), a chronic voyeur, cajoles a shoplifter into stripping for him by professing to be a proponent of 'Peep Art'.

These outwardly random pursuits nevertheless mesh to refute the picture of a contentedly complacent society as described by President Johnson at the beginning of the movie: "I'm not saying you never had it so good. But that's a fact, isn't it?" And much of *Greetings* is irresistibly comic: the friends' mock interviews with draft board officers (in rehearsal for the real thing), Paul pinning his hopes of rejection on flamboyant homosexual mannerisms and Fascistic rhetoric; the loony encounter with a street-corner revolutionary who believes that General Motors' imperialist ambitions are revealed in the name of its corporate headquarters, the Empire State Building; or Jon's elaborate pitch to induce the shoplifter to strip while, framed unnoticed in a window behind him, another young woman casually undresses. By the movie's end, however, paranoia has been fully vindicated as the sanest response to a society coming apart at the seams. Before meeting with his supposed Oswald witness, Paul himself is mysteriously shot; and Jon, whose paramilitary discourse, taken over from Paul, has — not entirely surprisingly — failed to deter the army, finds himself drafted to Vietnam, where he can freely indulge his voyeuristic proclivities: he forces a Vietnamese girl to strip for newsreel cameramen.

In 1970, DePalma completed a sequel, *Hi, Mom!* (the first word addressed to the TV cameras by a returning vet), in which Jon was once more prominently featured. *Greetings,* though hardly a major work, was even in its ungainliness manifestly more honest than all the slick inanities of those 'youth' movies whose widest generation gap was that which stretched between director and subject matter (e.g. John G. Avildsen's crudely opportunistic portrait of a hard-hat bigot, *Joe,* 1970, whose hippie characters appeared to be impersonated by plain-clothes detectives rather than actors, and Stanley Kramer's typically elephantine *RPM* — meaning 'Revolutions Per Minute' — made the same year). Draft resistance as a comic *motif* also surfaced in Bruce Kessler's *The Gay Deceivers* (1969): its two heroes, harassed by the embarrassment to their private lives caused by posing as homosexuals, finally resign themselves to enlisting — only to be rejected by the draft board officer and his aide, homosexuals themselves whose cherished ambition is of an exclusively gay army! And in Jack Nicholson's directorial debut, *Drive, He Said* (1971), a student 'guerilla' embarks on a crash program of heavy

Jon (Robert De Niro) rehearsing a madness act for the draft board. Paul (Jonathan Warden) and Lloyd (Gerritt Graham) look on – ***'GREETINGS'***

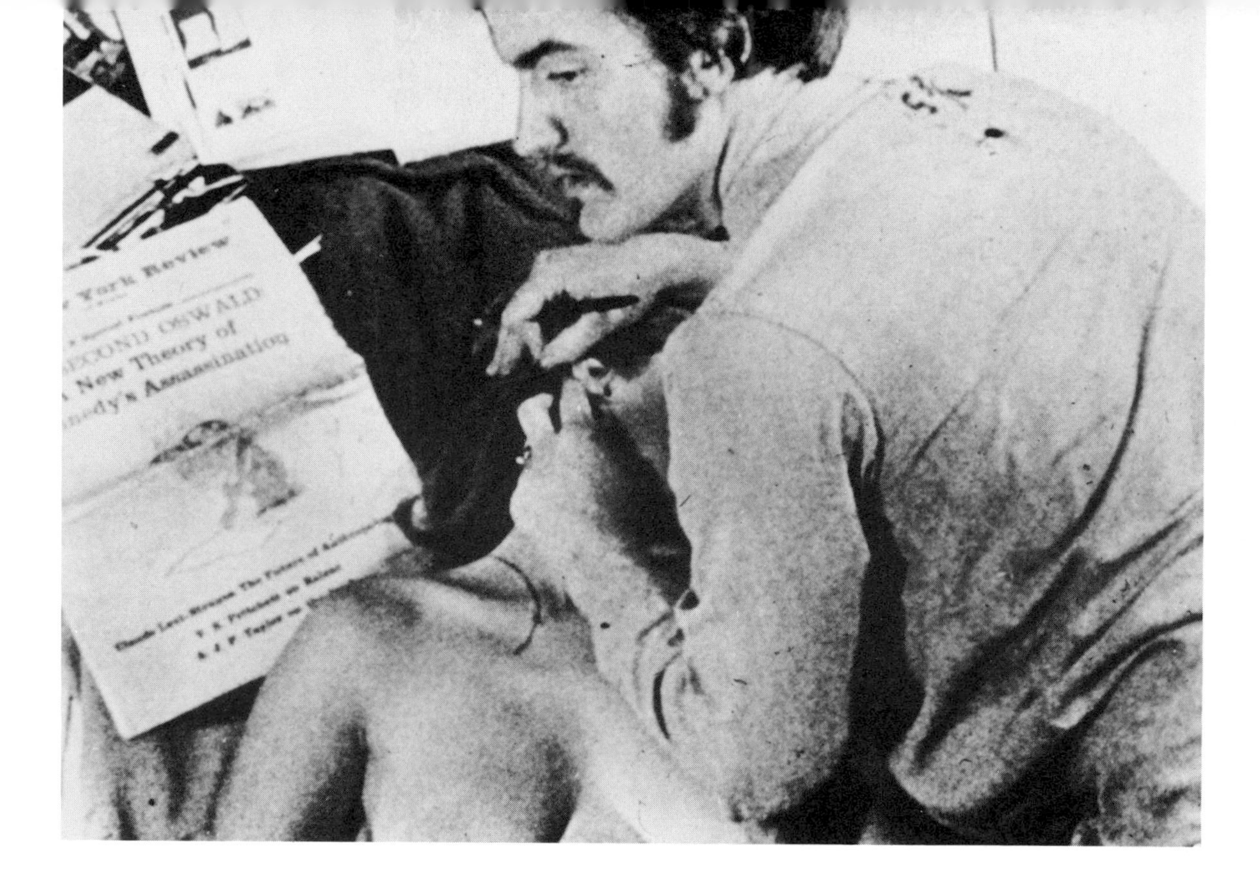

Lloyd obsessed with Lee Harvey Oswald tests a theory – ***'GREETINGS'***

drugs and sleepless nights in preparation for his pre-induction physical.

As the resistor began to acquire respectability, however, the cinema produced less frivolous treatments of his situation. When Joan Baez' husband, the activist David Harris, was sentenced shortly after their marriage to three years imprisonment for resisting the draft, a documentary film, *Carry It On* (1970, GB *Joan* — obviously to avoid confusion with the *Carry On...* series), recounted the couple's life together, his arrest and her subsequent concert tour. At the less charismatic end of the spectrum were two Canadian films, Robin Spry's unpretentious *Prologue* (1968) and Jules Bricken's cliché-ridden *Explosion* (1969), and Hiroshi Teshigahara's *Summer Soldiers* (1972), about a determinedly ordinary GI stationed in Japan, Jim (Keith Sykes), who casually chooses to desert rather than fight in Vietnam. In *cinéma verité* style, the movie follows his progress as an AWOL, from a clandestine sojourn in a prostitute's room (hiding in a cupboard whenever there is a knock at the door) to his involvement with the Tokyo Deserters Aid Committee (to whose ideological debates he is apathetically indifferent and whose request that he give a press conference on TV — as The Singing Deserter — he declines) via the nervous hospitality of a little network of Japanese families sympathetic to the deserters' cause. Finally, after an abortive attempt to work his passage on a ship bound for Sweden, Jim walks into the army base at Kyoto in the hope of obtaining an official discharge.

Peter Fonda and Lindsey Wagner in Robert Wise's ***'TWO PEOPLE'***

In its refusal to heighten the deserter's plight or draw hasty (or, indeed, any) conclusions from his abrupt decision to surrender, lie both the strengths and weaknesses of this intermittently fascinating film. So bland, so passive is Jim that he remains a cypher throughout, returning to the army as he had departed from it, almost as a whim — which rather belies the remark by one of the Aid Committee's earnest young idealists: "Desertion is meaningful in itself." One doesn't ask that the protagonist of such a movie be portentously 'representative' of all deserters, merely someone capable of bringing a degree of reflection to bear on his own predicament.

Though there were a number of marginal productions on the issue — Simon Nuchtern's *Cowards* (about deserters in Canada), Anitra Pivnik's *Prism* (about a lawyer who aids draft dodgers) and Allan Brown's *Outside In* (a deserter's homecoming to his father's funeral) — it was handled by no major studio until Robert Wise's pedestrian melodrama *Two People* (1975), which had the singular notion of exploiting the deserter's return home for a travelog tour *à la Three Coins in the Fountain* of the Soviet Union, North Africa and Paris. Other movies dealt with the less fashionable theme of young Americans (generally of rural origin) actually accepting, albeit reluctantly, to go fight for their country. The protagonist of David Miller's *Hail, Hero!* (1969) — played by Michael Douglas, son of Kirk and the future producer of *The China Syndrome* (1979) — volunteers for a disconnected joblot of reasons: out of respect for his World War II veteran father; because he had accidentally crippled his pro-war brother; and, perhaps, to confound the enemy with his own pacifist convictions ("What would happen if every soldier on both sides would just try to love instead of hate?"). And Anthony Newley's *Summertree* (1971) concerned a student (Douglas again) whose gradual disenchantment with his studies ironically results in his being drafted and killed in Vietnam.

More recently, the draft has become fodder for nostalgia, like the faded pressed Flower Power of *Hair.* In Rob Cohen's *A Small Circle of Friends* (1980), a mail-order catalog of 60s splendors and miseries as they affected the lives of three Harvard undergraduates (one girl, two boys), including pot, women's lib, the Weathermen, unconventional sexual mores and the token battle between cops and demonstrating students (in the Harvard Yard), it is highlighted in a scene where the friends anxiously await the 64,000 dollar classification number on that obscene TV quiz show, the draft lottery. As *Time* critic Richard Schickel aptly observed, it came "to seem less a movie than a picture history of an era — one of those tomes that offer a garble of familiar images held together by a pseudohistorical text".

But revolution was in the air, precisely where Paul Williams' *The Revolutionary* (1970, based on Hans Koningsberger's novel) was determined to keep it. In marked contrast to the strident topicality of the protest movies, it was set in an unspecified country "somewhere in the free world" at an unspecified moment in recent history. Unspecified countries, however, are much easier to construct verbally than visually (especially in view of contemporary cinema's dependence on natural locations): here, notwithstanding its jackbooted policemen and absence of traffic, the city was inescapably London, the actors' inflections ineradicably American, and the costumes (Jon Voigt in baggy trousers, floppy wide-brimmed hat and tight rimless spectacles) instantly recognizable as classic revolutionary wear to anyone who has read Conrad's *The Secret Agent* or *Under Western Eyes.* In fact, the movie's calm pursuit of metaphoric intemporality removed it so far from the telegenic razzle-dazzle of 60s campus rioting into an almost turn-of-the-century world of anarchist dreamers (one half-expected a big black bomb with a lighted fuse to be concealed beneath Voigt's shabby raincoat) that the political and moral issues which it raised seemed to be of historical, rather than universal or topical, import or else were

Carl Dixon (Michael Douglas) returns from a tour of duty to unwelcome adulation from parents and friends – ***'HAIL, HERO'***

Terry (Michael Douglas) fatally wounded in Vietnam – ***'SUMMERTREE'***

articulated in a void that no amount of Kafkaesque angst (Voigt's character is named simply 'A' — surely an exclusively literary conceit) could make resonate.

Robert Kramer, director of *The Edge* (1968), *Ice* (1969) and *Milestones* (1975), has many vociferous admirers (particularly in France), and there is no doubting his work's fundamental honesty of purpose. His films, made without (to my knowledge) any official harassment, nevertheless contrive to appear as objects of bureaucratic suspicion, as if smuggled out of some beleaguered totalitarian state. But they also founder on an oddly puritanical variant of the imitative fallacy, whereby any tedious incident, for the characters, is made no less so for the audience; political debates of stupefying banality (and frequently couched in a monosyllabic idiom guaranteed to make your toes curl with embarrassment) are served up raw, without much sign of directorial mediation; and nocturnal scenes (of which there are many in Kramer's work) are rendered virtually invisible by underexposed 16mm stock.

The Edge took as its subject an assassination attempt on the President in reparation for the slaughter in Vietnam, while *Ice* dealt with urban guerilla insurrection in an imagined period of war between the United States and Mexico (which could be interpreted as either a paranoid foretaste of the future course of America's imperialist expansion or as a metaphorical substitute for Vietnam itself). And at 206 minutes, *Milestones* (co-directed by John Douglas) was a mammoth orgy of melancholic self-questioning in which random groups of Americans of mostly WASP origin meet to discuss their lives, projects, ambitions and achievements in the light of their experience of the previous decade: these include an intellectual once imprisoned for aiding deserters, a war veteran, a student activist, a militant cell, some ex-dropouts, members of a commune and a baby who is born in the movie's final sequence. It is dedicated to Ho Chi Minh and the "heroic Vietnamese people".

The ultimate in *noir* cinema, Kramer's movies are pitch black (despite the affirmation of rebirth at the end of *Milestones);* all the more so because, eschewing the neo-expressionist stylistics of 40s thrillers, they risk striking the unwary spectator as straightforward, almost documentary recordings of a world that is objectively *noir.* But if they have in common with nightmares the quality of preternatural vividness, one finds it rather difficult, as also with nightmares, to recall them in detail when they are all over.

As for the New York Underground scene, its conceptualist preoccupations tended to preclude any urgent commitment to filming the war; the sole example of a Vietnam-related issue figuring in a linear narrative was Adolfas Mekas' *Windflowers* (1968) , about a draft dodger mercilessly tracked down and killed by the FBI. But vague allusions crop up in at least two Andy Warhol flicks: *Blue Movie* (1968), where the war represents only one link in a chain of free association chitchat between love-makers Louis Waldon and Viva (even if Warhol with forgivable disingenuousness defended the movie as 'about Vietnam' when it was prosecuted for obscenity), and *The Chelsea Girls* (1969), in which another Factory denizen, Mary Might, impersonated the sadistic 'Hanoi Hannah'... In several other movies, both from New York and Hollywood, Vietnam atrocities were to be glimpsed from television screens or overheard on car radios (as also in much European cinema of the period, e.g. the self-incinerating Buddhist monk in Bergman's *Persona,* 1971).

Non-American films do not really form part of this study, but one should mention *Loin du Viêtnam (Far from Vietnam,* 1967), collectively directed by Alain Resnais, William Klein, Joris Ivens, Agnes Varda, Claude Lelouch, Jean-Luc Godard and edited by Chris Marker. A curious ragbag in which quite good jostled indiscriminately with very bad, it too often resorted to effective but simplistic antinomies: General Westmoreland's outrageous assertion that "Never has a military nation employed its power with such restraint" offset by images of the obscene havoc wreaked by American bombing, Vice-President Humphrey's

A. (Jon Voight) Leonard II (Seymour Cassel), and Desford (Robert Duvall) discuss subterfuge – ***'THE REVOLUTIONARY'***

confident account of his state visit to Paris intercut with newsreel footage of angry demonstrators lining his path, etc. Godard used his section to accost the audience directly with a string of gnomic utterances on the difficulty for a European artist to make a statement about the war, a sentiment limply echoed by Resnais in a peculiarly thin-blooded playlet about an equivocating French intellectual.

Vietnam, of course, had always engaged Godard, from the brilliant pantomime sequence with Anna Karina in *Pierrot le Fou* (1965) to the fatuous moment in *Deux ou Trois Choses Que Je Sais d'Elle (Two or Three Things I Know About Her,* 1966 — a masterpiece, nevertheless) when Marina Vlady's child recalls his dream of twins on a perilous mountain path merging into one person to enable him to pass — "... and, at that moment, I discovered that these two people were North and South Vietnam..." In *La Chinoise* (1967) Godard invented for the cinema the political cartoon, with a coolie-hatted, blood-spattered Juliet Berto strafed by toy planes and, forming the background, a giant poster of the Esso tiger; in *Letter to Jane* (1972, co-directed by Jean-Pierre Gorin) he sought to analyze and demystify a press photograph of Jane Fonda in company with some North Vietnamese which had been published in the French news magazine *L'Express.* (Fonda herself was involved in a couple of documentaries, her own *Vietnam Journey* and Francine Parker's *F.T.A.* — either Free the Army or Fuck the Army — the cinematic record of an antiwar *USO* show and 'subversive' updating of the old Hollywood Canteen format.) Claude Lelouch's unsalvageably

An unequivocal message in Robert Kramer's ***'ICE'***

Jane Fonda in Hanoi –
'LETTER TO JANE'
(1972)

meretricious *Vivre Pour Vivre* (*Live For Life,* 1967), juxtaposing in true Sunday supplement manner newsreel images of war atrocities with Candice Bergen blithely riding through Central Park at dawn, added to the period's list of chic jet-setting professions — fashion photographer, international racing driver — that of TV reporter in Vietnam, and ex-cinematographer Raoul Coutard shot his *Hoâ-Binh* (1970) in what one imagines to be just the visual style favored by Lelouch's glamorous hero.

But it was also in 1970 that Metro-Goldwyn-Mayer, the studio which had once been Hollywood's center-court, the temple and bastion of traditional Middle America values, released Stuart Hagmann's *The Strawberry Statement* (based by dramatist Israel Horowitz on James Simon Kunen's *The Strawberry Statement: Notes of a College Revolutionary).* The movie, whose incongruous title refers to the university dean's claim that students were against the war in much the same casually Pavlovian way they liked strawberries, traces the gradual politicization of young, fence-sitting Simon (played by Bruce Davison with irritating winsomeness throughout), who almost stumbles into the protest movement after being mildly aggressed by the police ("What is this — France?") for taking photographs of the campus sit-in, and his on-off-on relationship with the more committed Linda (Kim Darby). And it's perhaps a measure of Hagmann's personal remoteness from the lived experience of campus unrest that the movie's visual surfaces seem to have been as lavishly reconstructed as for a period melodrama. This is the nostalgia of 'now'.

In the opening sequence, when Simon comes home to find his room-mate in bed with a girl involved in the occupation of the college administration buildings, the slowly tracking camera

Claude Lelouch's ***'VIVRE POUR VIVRE'***

'parenthetically' encounters in its field of vision such archetypal 60s bric-a-brac as a poster photograph of Robert Kennedy, a signpost stolen from the City Zoo, some San Francisco-ish sidewalk pottery, a pair of jeans laid out to dry on the window ledge — in fact, all heavy clues to the protagonist's life-style as carefully planted by the set designer as the football pennant, baseball mittens and Lana Turner pin-up of an earlier generation. Spying a cockroach, he remarks: "You guys are everywhere, you're like the Viet Cong." In the Bay Area streets he never *walks,* he idly moons around, transfixed in the shimmer of a wide-angle lens; a cart loaded with groceries 'poetically' runs away with him (a scene influenced by the Redford/Newman cycling antics in *Butch Cassidy and the Sundance Kid,* which had already been vulgarly cribbed from *Jules et Jim);* and when assigned by the student council to fix the administration's Xerox machine, he cutely wastes time by applying the principal's shaving cream and aftershave to his (canned) peaches-and-cream complexion. Plus countless similar hints that his youthful insouciance is due to receive some violent political come-uppance in the final reel (as indeed it proves).

The movie could have provided a useful gloss on the mechanics of a student occupation — demonstrators sneaking out just before dark to obtain food supplies, the local grocer (James Coco) urging them to pillage the most expensive delicacies in his store so that he can claim theft insurance, the sudden eagerness of Simon's friend Elliot (Bud Cort) to join the protest on hearing that among those sequestered inside the principal's office are 150 girls — but the modish curlicues of Hagmann's maddeningly fidgety camerawork render it well nigh unintelligible. With its slow motion, freeze frames, excessive focus-pulling, 'artistic' dissolves and ubiquitous zoom shots, *The Strawberry Statement* is abominably shot. Never for a moment is the spectator permitted to engage directly with the characters, who have to contend with a barrage of arty camera angles as much as with the 'pigs' themselves. And the redundancy of these effects is compounded by the tenuousness of their links with the narrative: Simon's rowing practice for the college team, an activity which by the end of the movie he can no longer reconcile with his militancy, is treated to a series of lyrically slow dissolves in which his skiff lazily crisscrosses itself on the sparkling river, whereas the participants of the sit in, with whom the director's sympathies presumably lie, are filmed (and played) with an almost caricatural lack of warmth. It becomes increasingly clear, moreover, that the various romantic interludes and campus in-fighting are serving merely as a protracted build-up to the final sequence, a spectacular police bust, which is to this movie what, for example, the San Francisco car chase was to *Bullitt.*

Watching this setpiece, visibly choreographed to within an inch of its life, I was reminded of another, ostensibly very dissimilar movie. *Footlight Parade* was a Warner Bros. backstage musical directed in 1933 by Lloyd Bacon and starring James Cagney, Dick Powell and Ruby Keeler. Briefly, its plot is the one about impresario Cagney putting on a Broadway show (in fact, prologues, i.e. stage presentations which in the 30s preceded the screening of a feature film) against numerous, mostly financial odds; but what makes it, to my mind, the best of Warners'

Lelouch's ***'VIVRE POUR VIVRE'***

extravaganzas of the period is its unusual construction. Until the final explosion of no fewer than *three* Busby Berkeley numbers, magnificent revolving Catherine Wheels of feminine limbs framed in his celebrated overhead shots, we have been privy to no more than glimpses of musical numbers, frustratingly truncated and generally in rehearsal. In fact, the whole movie consists of rehearsals — for the duration of which, it should be noted, the chorus girls and boys are *locked* inside the theater — in preparation for its triple climax. To employ a sexual metaphor (and Berkeley's career has triumphantly borne out the equation between musical spectacle and eroticism), after a lengthy bout of foreplay *Footlight Parade* 'comes' three times.

This is precisely how *The Strawberry Statement* functions: the only confrontation between cops and protestors prior to the main event, a confused skirmish in the neighborhood playground which happens to be the students' immediate point of contention (they believe it should be given over to children from the black ghetto), is shot with a clownish disregard for realism. The cathartic release of real violence — we understand — is being saved for the end. When the students finally learn — suspense, suspense — that the helmeted and gas-masked National Guard have surrounded the administration buildings, they arrange themselves in circles on the gym floor and begin to sing in unison.

Authority re-established in the final scene of Stuart Hagmann's ***'THE STRAWBERRY STATEMENT'*** *- shades of Busby Berkeley.*

As the student occupation of the campus ends, Simon (Bruce Davison) finds commitment at last in the same movie.

And lo! what does Hagmann then do but revert to the overhead shot: the Busby Berkeley resemblance is complete (though, given that they are chanting Lennon's Johnny-one-note lyric "Give Peace a Chance", the earlier film is *musically* far superior). The actual melée, with clouds of tear gas prettily disturbing the symmetry of the concentric circles and Guardsmen lashing out indiscriminately and with totally unjustified savagery, would have been more impressive if its luridly bloody display of police brutality had not so patently been the sole reason for a studio as conformist as MGM getting involved with the project in the first place. Here the movie indubitably 'comes'.

In one of his essays in *The Primal Screen,* the American critic Andrew Sarris claimed that Hagmann's original intention, reversed by studio boss James Aubrey, was that Simon be killed at the end; in the version released, he is caught in a freeze frame as he lurches to aid Linda. Sarris (who was vaguely sympathetic toward the film) went on to remark: "The movie is set in some anonymous institution in the San Francisco Bay area without being either Berkeley (the historical continuity of radicalism) or San Francisco State (the sudden eruption of black power with muscle). Why? (...) The book is about Columbia, and no student was killed at Columbia by the police bust." Which all rather makes one wonder which was the more crassly opportunistic decision:

*Lecturer Harry Bailey (Elliott Gould) finally breaks with tradition – **'GETTING STRAIGHT'***

to end the movie with a killing or to suppress that killing.

"We'll go to the aquarium and turn on with the fish like we used to." So one of his ex-girlfriends importunes Harry Bailey (Elliott Gould) at the beginning of Richard Rush's *Getting Straight,* the other campus movie produced by a major studio in 1970. But Harry, who served both at Selma and in Vietnam, is through with political agitation: his sole ambition is to complete his MA and earn a teaching credential, whose attractions he succinctly summarizes to a black militant friend as "money and power and little girls to molest". (Its disadvantages include a practice course of what is disparagingly referred to as "dumbbell English" — teaching college students to make short sentences with the present participle of the verb 'to be'!) Torn between the demands being made on his activist past and an exasperation with new computerized teaching methods which may well affect his future, his own personal revolt comes at an oral exam where a rather sweatily insistent professor attempts to force him into agreement on what he sees as the latent homosexuality of *The Great Gatsby* and its author. While outside protestors and National Guard have finally clashed, Harry, by impudently kissing this professor on the mouth, effectively kisses an academic career goodbye.

A minor, occasionally witty comedy-drama, *Getting Straight* succeeds where Harry failed: in keeping campus revolution safely in the background (for no precise motivation is ever attributed to the rioting). Its final images, with Harry and his current girlfriend (Candice Bergen), their respective identity crises now definitively

resolved, exchanging worldly smirks as around them surges an exotic mass of youthful humanity, is pure love-across-a-crowded-room sentimentality. And not even Elliott Gould's prodigious mongrel charm can prevent his valedictory line "It's not what you do that counts, it's what you are" (addressed to the black militant while the latter is gleefully smashing in windows) from sounding as trite and reactionary as, for example, "Love means never having to say you're sorry". Well, almost as trite.

Nostalgia for the 60s. Treat Williams and his unwilling partner, Charlotte Rae, at the wedding – ***'HAIR'***

SECTION IV

RETURN OF THE SON OF VIETNAM

THE ENDING of the Vietnam war knew no '20s'. To clarify: after World War I, a conflict comparable to Vietnam in the widespread revulsion which overtook the event long before the Armistice was signed, in the overwhelming sense of useless slaughter suffered on both sides and in the gradual realization that it constituted a dramatic and truly qualitative break in the nation's history, the United States plunged into a period of isolationism and political apathy that lasted until the Depression. This was the semi-mythical era of jazz, flappers and bathtub gin (paradoxically enlivened further by the advent of Prohibition), of the celebrated Lost Generation (no less paradoxically, a term invariably used to describe the victors of the war) and of a compulsive, even neurotic urge to live, love, laugh and be happy 'for yesterday we died'.

But the aftermath of Vietnam granted its survivors no such release, perhaps because the contiguous 'roaring' decade was this time *concurrent* with the war: rock was the 60s jazz, boys grew their hair long just as girls had once bobbed theirs to dissociate themselves from their elders, earnest communal living projects supplanted the legendary sexual promiscuity of the 20s and the legal interdiction on drugs had precisely the same effect on drug-taking as Prohibition on the consumption of alcohol. Even in movies where the relation of Vietnam to the narrative remained a strictly exploitative one, Hollywood with remarkable

Angry vet solidarity – ***'WINTER SOLDIER'***

consistency portrayed the returning veteran as incurably 'changed', almost as much an 'alien' as the faceless enemy with whom he had been in contact. Though not necessarily 'disturbed' in a clinical sense, and often judged capable of functioning in society without the purgatory of hospitalization, he was depicted as somehow not the same person — mentally or physically (or both) — who had departed for the war. Consequently, all 'returning vet' movies (which are surprisingly numerous in Hollywood's treatment of Vietnam-related themes) may be said to be paraphrases of Huston's still unseen *Let There Be Light.*

Winter Soldier (1972, no director credited) was an edited record of the Winter Soldier Investigation held in Detroit in January, 1971. It was organised by the Vietnam Veterans Against the War (a group whose membership grew continuously after its formation in 1967), and during three days of hearings sixteen civilians and over one hundred veterans (all of them, it should be noted, *honorably* discharged) testified, publicly though not under any oath, to war crimes either witnessed or committed by them in Vietnam — twenty-eight of which the movie documents. These include the splitting open of infants' heads with cans of food for which they were begging, the dropping of live prisoners from helicopters and the rape of a dying woman with an entrenchment tool. That for obvious reasons the movie can offer little in the way of visual evidence to support this testimony (though one of the witnesses had consented to be photographed in the act of torturing a woman) in no way diminishes its power: men who were self-confessed killers *then* we see, in agonizing close-ups, to be ordinary God-fearing, if profoundly disturbed, citizens *now,* painfully straining (many are poorly educated) to articulate the warped rationale behind their crimes.

Poster – ***'CHROME AND HOT LEATHER'***

But — and this is where it most strikingly differs from a documentary like *Let There Be Light* – *Winter Soldier* does not merely aim at providing a filmic record of what was visibly a therapeutic experience, it *is* that experience. Here film has been commandeered by the 'patients' themselves as a medium of expiation, a confessional, and one would like to hope that the participants in this unique experiment have, if not eased the burden of their conscience, at least in some measure adjusted to bearing that burden, as they must, for the rest of their lives. Unlike Huston's movie, *Winter Soldier* was not suppressed — it was, in fact, widely screened on the university circuit — as if in half-official recognition that these hearings, as well as the atrocities which they brought to light, formed a regrettable but inevitable part of the 'tragedy' of Vietnam.

In the late 60s, exploitation movies were still following in the deeply rutted motorcycle tracks mapped out by *The Wild One* and its successors, and the integration of Vietnam into this iconography was usually achieved at little cost to the original concept. All it required was to attribute the hero's antisocial disposition, not to the traumatic withdrawal of parental love as in the 50s but to the collective trauma (as it was already being referred to) of the war. As if to guarantee a veneer of 'significance', allusion would be made to Vietnam in the first few minutes of the movie, which then happily settled for the customary diet of crude trigger-happy violence.

Bruce Kessler's *Angels From Hell* (1968), for example, concerned a vet returning to wrest leadership of his old bike gang from the non-combatant who had replaced him for the duration. (Kessler approached the theme of Vietnam from a somewhat different angle in his 'caught in the draft' comedy *The Gay Deceivers.)* Al Adamson's *Satan's Sadists* (1969) modified the formula slightly by setting its brutal vet hero in conflict with a motorcycle gang: to quote from a plot synopsis, "he utilizes his combat training by smashing a mirror in the face of one of the thugs and drowning another in a toilet bowl". It therefore took no more than that toilet bowl to assure the movie a place in the filmography of Vietnam. Whereas, in Jack Starrett's decidedly more inventive *The Losers* (1971), Link (William Smith), the brother of a high-ranking military official, is dispatched *to* Cambodia with four spaced-out motorcyclist friends (whose freaky names — Duke, Speed, Limpy and Dirty Denny — are faintly reminiscent of the Seven Dwarfs) to rescue an American Presidential Adviser from a Chinese prison camp. Though ostensibly anti-Establishment in outlook (albeit in a vein of right wing anarchism most profitably exploited by Aldrich's *The Dirty Dozen,* 1966), this thoroughly dislikeable movie transferred the aesthetics of the 'action replay' from sport to war by treating the spectator to frequent bouts of slow-motion slaughter as the gang, to quote from publicity material, "do their special thing for the US Army". The same press handout also optimistically claimed for

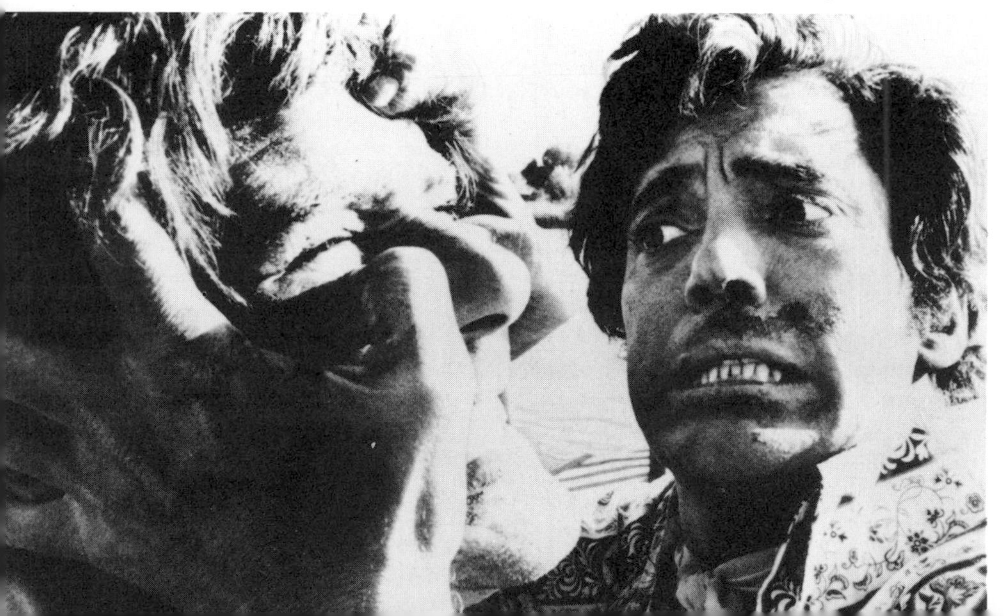

*Phil (Robert Fuller) fights his way out of a tough situation – **'THE HARD RIDE'***

Phil and Sheryl (Sherry Bain) on the super chopper – **'THE HARD RIDE'**

the movie: "The result of their attempt and the mission provide a capsule of what the Vietnam conflict is all about for confused Americans — from fighting the unseen enemy to living with the results of a battle too costly to be called a victory, and too complex and frustrating to result in the human glory that comes from having won."

Chrome and Hot Leather (1971 directed by Lee Frost) involved four ex-Green Beret instructors (viewed sympathetically throughout) who, to avenge the killing of their leader's fiancée by a Hell's Angel, amass an improbable arsenal of tear gas, rockets, smoke grenades, explosion simulators, not to mention assorted radios, walkie-talkies, field rations and a command post tent. It was perhaps the most risibly extreme illustration of themes that were constantly to recur in this cycle of films: the illusory nature of 'peace' for the returning veteran, the blurring of the distinction between Vietnam and gang warfare at home, the effectiveness of combat training as a 'street savvy' course for survival in the urban jungle of contemporary America. And when the protagonist of Burt Topper's *The Hard Ride* (1970), returning from Vietnam with the body of his black buddy, himself ended up as part of a double burial, a specious connection was patently being forged between the two casualties.

Non-motorcycle variants on the same basic recipe were Alex March's *The Big Bounce* (1968), which gave Ryan O'Neal his first starring role as a misfit vet drifting helplessly into criminality, Jack Haley Jr's *Norwood* (1969), a soft-centered comedy about a vet's rise to Country-and-Western stardom, with Glen Campbell, Kim Darby (later of *The Strawberry Statement),* Dom De Luise, baseball star Joe Namath and the director's father Jack Haley Sr

Studied malevolence – ***'THE BORN LOSERS'***

(once the Tin Man in *The Wizard of Oz),* and Richard Sarafian's *Vanishing Point* (1971, from a scenario by the noted Cuban novelist Guillermo Cabrera Infante, pseudonymously credited as 'Guillermo Cain'), a road movie whose ex-Marine, ex-cop, ex-racing driver protagonist, "the last beautiful free soul on this planet", whimsically accepts a wager to drive a supercharged Dodge Challenger at top speed from Denver to San Francisco only to meet his death at an impassable roadblock.

After the systematic 'blaxploitation' of the thriller and horror genres, it was just a question of time before the first black veteran, 'utilizing the skills he learned in Vietnam, etc', would stalk across the screen. As a government agent explains to the eponymous hero (played by former athlete Jim Brown) of Jack Starrett's *Slaughter* (1972): "You're a Green Beret and you're black. That's good copy." Such good copy, in fact, that two years later a sequel, Gordon Douglas's *Slaughter's Big Rip-Off,* was laboriously squeezed out of the same tube. And in 1972 Jim Brown turned up as the equally invincible *Black Gunn* (directed by Robert Hartford-Davis), on this occasion avenging his brother's murder with the aid of BAG — a Black Action Group composed of Vietnam veterans.

More pretentious, if hardly more ambitious, was *The Born Losers* (1967), directed by its leading man, Tom Laughlin, under the *nom de caméra-stylo* of T. C. Frank. Laughlin, however, is a special case, an enigmatic young moviemaker messianically convinced that he holds the key to America's spiritual re-generation, a conviction doubtless reinforced (for him) by the phenomenal box-office returns of what was basically a high-budget home movie (and those of its glossier sequels, *Billy Jack, The Trial of Billy Jack* and *Billy Jack goes to Washington,* all marketed under Laughlin's aegis following his dissatisfaction with the way Columbia-Warner had handled the distribution of *Billy Jack).* Its protagonist, now something of a folk hero, is a sullen half-breed veteran who grapples singlehandedly with almost every major problem to have beset the nation over the last two decades — urban violence, racial prejudice, the Indian question, political chicanery and the defense of alternative lifestyles. In the face of such a cannonade of virtuous bloodletting, with Billy Jack meting out karate chops to a motley selection of villians, one is tempted to comment that not since Tet and the notorious American claim that "We had to destroy the city in order to save it" has there been such a shotgun wedding of brutish methods and pacifist motives (with the officiating minister preaching the opposite of what he practises).

Martin Scorsese once situated Travis Bickle, the psychopathic hero (played by Robert De Niro) of his movie *Taxi Driver,* as "somewhere between Charles Manson and Saint Paul". (But aren't we all?) Bickle, an ex-Vietnam Marine plagued with insomnia, drives his taxi on night-shift while his days are spent either scribbling lapidary reflections into a diary or pursuing a frosty upper class blonde in the shape of Cybill Shepherd. In search of some civic mission by which the corrosive rage of his alienation might be exorcised, he decides against assassinating the Presidential candidate for whom the blonde is campaigning and befriends an underage junkie prostitute (Jodie Foster), whose pimp and his associates he will eventually slaughter in an outstandingly violent bloodbath. Exemplified by a mesmerizing first shot of a yellow cab lurching in slow-motion through nocturnal neon-lit streets to Bernard Herrmann's overripe score while clouds of vapor luridly billow from a manhole as from the kitchens of Hell, Scorsese's ghoulish vision of New York City (and he correctly hit on *red,* a sanguine red filling every vacant pocket of the frame, as the dominant tonality of a *film noir* in color) is as stylized as a movie poster and bizarrely reminiscent — in

Billy Jack (Tom Laughlin) deals out his own brand of justice – ***'BILLY JACK'***

advance, so to speak — of Coppola's brooding jungle landscapes in *Apocalypse Now.* If *Taxi Driver* is not explicitly 'about' Vietnam, if Scorsese and his screenwriter Paul Shrader never sufficiently articulate Bickle's neuroses to tie them in with his combat experience, there are nevertheless numerous angles from which it looks suspiciously like a parable of the war (or Coppola's version of it).

For all his animal physicality, Bickle is as wraithlike a figure as Martin Sheen's Willard: gliding through their respective jungles, they repulse audience identification as they invite it by suddenly turning their accusatory gaze on the spectator, a disorienting effect achieved with functional smoothness in *Taxi Driver* since Bickle is obliged to scrutinize his unsavory passengers (who include Scorsese himself as a jealous husband intent on blowing his wife's vagina apart with a 44 Magnum) through his cab's rear view mirror, i.e. directly into camera. Determined to reach a peak of physical fitness for his chosen 'mission', he inflicts strict military discipline on himself even to the point of shaving his head guerilla-style and slapping on war paint. Shots of him posed in front of a mirror and repeatedly drawing a bead on his own reflection recall Sheen hovering between nightmarish reality and straight nightmare at the beginning of Coppola's film. His climatic raid on the brothel, if necessarily bereft of the sacrificial symbolism surrounding Brando's death in *Apocalypse Now,* is still presented almost ceremoniously, both a ritualized self-purging and cleansing of pollution, as witness the way he grasps

Director Martin Scorcese is Travis' passenger – ***'TAXI DRIVER'***

Travis makes his first strike as vigilante, gunning down a petty thief.

the Magnum firmly with both hands and at arm's length, a posture familiar from those movie apologies of urban vigilantes played by Clint Eastwood or Charles Bronson. But *Taxi Driver* offers us no assurance as we delight in its graphic violence that Bickle, like so many other movie vets, is somehow 'infecting' America; the blackness of Scorsese's vision easily matches that of his protagonist and his picture of a festering New York, with manholes like open sores, often seems to detach itself from the subjectivity of Bickle's paranoid fantasies to become the movie's objective reality.

Significantly, its coda is every bit as ambiguous as that of *Apocalypse Now,* as if neither director knew how to bring his movie to a satisfactory conclusion. We gather from a magazine clipping pinned to the wall in his squalid room that Bickle has been acclaimed as a civic hero, and even the cool blonde warms toward his freshly acquired macho image. Though racist and misogynistic and sometimes downright silly, *Taxi Driver* remains a curious object to have been manufactured in Hollywood (where from its inception it was considered an extremely risky project) and one unlikely to have emerged in quite the form it did, had there not been that war rumbling away on the other side of the globe.

Not all veterans — even in the movies — would replace their pent-up violence by such all-out assaults on whatever threatened the purity of the system they had been enlisted to defend. There existed concurrently with these thrillers a more intimate strain, one which confined the problem of the returning vet to relatively modest narrative dimensions and a closed, often rural space. It

Iris (Jodie Foster), the junkie prostitute and the focus of Travis' paternal feelings – ***'TAXI DRIVER'***

was launched in 1971 with Edwin Sherin's *Glory Boy* (rereleased under the title of John Sanford's original World War I novel, *My Old Man's Place),* about an ex-serviceman, tormented by the memory of atrocities he committed in Vietnam, who returns with two other soldiers to his father's isolated farmhouse in Northern California. A conveniently unfocused indictment of the brutalizing effects of war, it fatally undermined its thesis by filming the resultant brutalities — the visit culminates in rape and murder — with undisguised relish.

A year later, the first Vietnam movie by a generally acknowledged major director, Elia Kazan's *The Visitors* (from an original screenplay by his son Chris), was to make use of a not dissimilar plot. Shot by a five-man non-union crew on location in the director's own house in Connecticut, with a cast of unknowns and a derisory budget of 170,000 dollars, it concerned a sensitive young veteran, now a confirmed pacifist, who lives with his girlfriend and their infant son in a New England farmhouse owned by her father, a middle-aged alcoholic writer of pulp Western

Travis and Wizard (Peter Boyle) – just another night.

novels. Without warning they are visited one day by two army buddies, a polite, easy-going black and a clean-cut, if somewhat intense, white sergeant — both of whom had been convicted of raping and murdering a Vietnamese girl on the evidence of their friend. Just out of Leavenworth penitentiary — closely cropped hair a grim holdover from prison rather than military rigors — their presence at first seems to forebode no specific thirst for vengeance. But time passes. They kill a neighbor's dog; learning that the pacifist declined to participate in the gang rape, the leathery old writer, himself a cheerfully uncomplexed veteran of the Pacific war, admits that he always suspected him of being "half-queer"; finally, they rape the young woman (an act overly telegraphed throughout the movie by the sergeant's insistent leering at her knees) and depart almost as casually as they had arrived.

A strange film, typically Kazanian in its moral and psychological ambiguities: via the pacifist's remorseful self-questioning "The Viet Cong do exactly the same thing. Everybody does. Why blame those guys? They were my friends, my buddies" and the sympathy gradually generated by the two visitors, it shifts by degrees from apparently endorsing the ethics of informing (and, irrelevantly *ad hominem* as this may be, it's impossible not to recall in the context the director's own cooperation with the

Travis gunning for Iris' pimp.

anti-Communist witchhunters of the early 50s) to apparently condoning war crimes. I say "apparently" because, though the movie is masterfully crafted in its atmospherics — the lonely farmhouse, the uneasily plausible blend of intangible Martian otherness and all-American affability in the rapists (taken to its logical conclusion in Bob Clark's *Dead of Night*, 1972, whose traumatized vet becomes a Zombie) — the two Kazans never stand back far enough from the double-edged material to avoid being instilled with their characters' indecisions. And I'm afraid Andrew Sarris did have a point when he commented (a propos *The Visitors* and movies of its type): " The problem is that the characters are all so awesomely awful that they don't really need Vietnam as an excuse to scrape on each other."

In Richard Compton's *Welcome Home, Soldier Boys* (1974), an account of four vets who set out full of illusions for California but end up in the no hope township of Hope, New Mexico, a grizzled farmer in a Texas diner mumbles: "When *we* were in the service, nobody came back till the war was *over*... Now they put in a coupla easy months and they come back and nothing's done. No wonder that damn war's gone on for ten years — oughta get the *old* army back there... Shit! You watch television — all they do is kill the damn civilians!" And a theme common to almost all these movies is the utter alienation of young people — whether draft card burners, deserters or veterans — from the elders of the tribe, who seem blessed with total recall of their own combat experiences, mnemonically revived from time to time by dusting off old and cherished army uniforms (as do the gung ho fathers, both played by Arthur Kennedy, of *Hail, Hero!* and *Glory Boy*). If we are to believe Hollywood, it was mainly nostalgia for the simple no-nonsense heroics of World War II that kept the generations so decisively divided over Vietnam.

Very occasionally, this alienation would surface in paranoid allegory or near-allegory (or whatever the moviemakers imagined they were up to). *Clay Pigeon* (GB. *Trip to Kill*, directed in 1971 by Tom Stern and Lane Slate) opens in Vietnam with ex-policeman Joe Ryan (played by Stern) heroically hurling his body onto an enemy grenade, which inexplicably fails to explode. Discharged and disenchanted, Joe returns to Los Angeles convinced he is living on borrowed time. There he is engulfed against his will in an obscure imbroglio of drugs and thuggery until the moment when, after slaying a trio of gangsters, he finds himself mysteriously transplanted back to Vietnam just as, presumably a second or two

Violence flares as Harry Wayne (Patrick McVey) comes to grips with guest Tony Rodriguez (Chico Martinez), Billy Schmidt (James Woods) looks on – ***'THE VISITORS'***

No hope heroes —
'WELCOME HOME SOLDIER BOYS'

after his suicidal gesture, the grenade explodes. Unfortunately, in so updating the ingenious conceit of Ambrose Bierce's *conte cruel* of the Civil War, *Incident at Owl Creek,* the movie forfeits all credibility by the preposterous convolutions of the plot inside which, for some unfathomable reason, Joe has elected to spend the last instant of his earthly existence.

Welcome Home, Johnny Bristol directed by George McCowans, a television film made in 1972, opened in Hollywood's familiar register of anecdotal naturalism, then seemed to veer off into allegorical fantasy before resolving itself as naturalistically as it had begun. To preserve his sanity in the bedlam of the war, Bristol (Martin Landau) calls up fond memories of an idyllic, affluent childhood in his home town of Charles, Vermont. On his return to the States, however, he discovers not only that no such community exists but that he was born in a slum area of Philadelphia at the intersection of Charles and Vermont Streets, whose names he had subconsciously conflated into an idealized America, one for which he was readier to risk his neck.

And in Henry Jaglom's *Tracks* (1976) Dennis Hopper played sergeant Jack Falen, assigned to accompany to its final resting place a coffin whose occupant he variously describes as his best friend, an anonymous hero or a black who saved his life in combat. As his train winds eastward across the bountiful geography of the country for which he fought and his friend died, the somewhat eccentric assortment of passengers encountered *en route* come to seem the fragmented reflections of its most recent history (it is

1973 and American involvement in Vietnam has just been formally terminated), as filtered through his own mental instability: an easy-going political activist, two ingenuously candid young girls off on holiday, a gregarious real estate dealer and his chess-playing companion. But when his rambling Vietnam reminiscences are met with responses ranging from indifference to pity, he breaks down completely — at which point it becomes clear that his sense of betrayal over the war is only part of a heavier burden of guilt and deprivation that he has borne since his childhood (one of his earliest memories is of sheepishly peeking at his mother's garters). That Falen is an emblematic figure, bearing the loss of national innocence on his frail shoulders (and there is a haunting rightness to the notion that Vietnam's Unknown Soldier should be one of its survivors) is confirmed by the film's ending (of a type that discourages interpretation since any single reading of it can doubtless be matched by others just as valid): leaping into the grave alongside the coffin, he re-emerges draped in the military gear that, it transpires, is all it contained.

Betrayal is still the theme of Jeremy Paul Kagen's *Heroes* (1977) and Karel Reisz's *Dog Soldiers* (1978), though what has been defiled is not childhood 'innocence' but the illusions of a period endowed — at least, from the vantage point of the decade that succeeded it — with the energy and fragile optimism of childhood: the 60s. The ebullient hero of *Heroes*, escaping from a psychiatric hospital where he is undergoing treatment after service in Vietnam (and there's a hint of bargain basement Jack Nicholson about Henry Winkler's characterization), sets out with the pooled savings of his fellow inmates to found a worm farm in California. Though adversity stalks his path — a violent run-in with muggers, the discovery that a buddy he hoped to enrol into his scheme was a war casualty, a painful moment of self-realization in Eureka, Cal. (the United States is apparently dotted with small towns whose names lend themselves to facile symbolism) — all will end happily for the Fonz in the softly comforting arms of a pretty girl.

Not so for the tormented protagonists of *Dog Soldiers* (based on the novel by Robert Stone, who collaborated on two separate

Joe Ryan (Tom Stern) 'living on borrowed time' —***CLAY PIGEON (G.B. 'TRIP TO KILL')***

versions of the script before withdrawing from further active participation in the project and subsequently disowning the completed film): they inject the poison of Vietnam — in the form of a cache of heroin — into the vulnerably fat American forearm. The movie's credit titles unroll over some nightmarish images of the war, which, though projected at normal speed, are shot in such a way as to invest the frenzied, directionless movement with something of the heavy, mastodonic sluggishness of slow-motion. A horrified witness to this explosive Armageddon, war correspondent John Converse (the excellent Michael Moriarty) forthwith arranges for a large shipment of heroin to be smuggled out of Vietnam. Not the least of the film's narrative inconsistencies,

Sgt. Jack Falen (Dennis Hopper) and Stephanie (Taryn Power) in an encounter on a train – ***'TRACKS'***

Jack Dunne (Henry Winkler) on the run from himself and the mental hospital – ***'HEROES'***

A loss of temper in the pool room ***'HEROES'***

however, is its failure to provide this moral and political volte face with any plausible motivation: it's never clear whether his decision is a gratuitous one, or made solely for profit, or from a whimsically formulated wish to measure up personally to the insanity of the war (as US Army helicopters circle the jungle, he comments offscreen: "In a world where elephants are pursued by flying men, people naturally want to get high").

The navy friend to whom he entrusts the mission, Ray (Nick Nolte), is first seen playing a game of football so mud-bespattered as hardly to differ from the war itself. Initially reluctant, Ray leaves for America and manages to smuggle the heroin out of the Oakland shipyards; but when he delivers it as instructed to Converse's wife Marge (Tuesday Weld), he discovers that she knows nothing of the operation. Whereupon *Dog Soldiers* develops into a fairly conventional chase movie in which Ray and Marge (her child packed off to relatives) are pursued through California by a pair of clownishly sadistic thugs hired by a crooked Narcotics Bureau agent. The war surfaces intermittently and in increasingly improbable places. The barbiturate-addicted Marge, for example, works in a protest bookshop. (So what?) When torturing Converse for information, the thugs switch on television to cover his screams — and, of course, it would have to be a news report from Vietnam. Reisz, an English director of Czech origin, has a tourist's tendency to allow the glittery idiosyncrasies of the American landscape to carry too much ideological weight: the fact that naked go-go dancers have invaded the bar which was Ray's favorite watering hole before his drafting seems a risibly lightweight indictment of a society's decline.

In its final sequence, the movie shifts gear into melancholic "Where have all the flowers gone" nostalgia as the two fugitives (Marge now dipping into the heroin) retreat to a fairy-lit Jesuit settlement in New Mexico which was once a hippie commune. There Ray sacrifices himself for Marge and Converse, who give him almost a soldier's burial by the roadside, with the heroin scattered over his grave as part of the ritual. As an oblique investigation into the effects of Vietnam on the American psyche, *Dog Soldiers* is not without its merits (notably Robert H. Kline's fluid and smokily beautiful photography), but is fatally compromised by Reiss's misguided determination to confine the war within the fussy, catch-all notion of a 'trauma', seeping insidiously into every crevice — and the film is mostly concerned with crevices — instead of coming to terms with how it irreparably altered the *whole* nation's perspective on its traditional values and aspirations.

In Ted Post's jejune potboiler, *Good Guys Wear Black* (1977), the element of betrayal, bathetically, never rises above the trusty old double-cross variety. Its hero, John T. Booker (played — if that's the word I'm looking for — by ex-karate champion Chuck Norris), attempts to discover who it was that set him up along with his "Black Tigers" commando unit during a raid to rescue CIA personnel from a Vietnamese fortress at the tail end of the war (as cease-fire conditions were being negotiated in Paris). Though now earning an unlikely living in California as a lecturer in political science ("The reasons for the war were beyond any kind

Correspondent and photographer John Converse (Michael Moriarty) – ***'DOG SOLDIERS'***

of logic" he announces to his spellbound class as the definitive word on Vietnam then, as if he had said something subversive, facetiously suggests they all sing patriotic songs), Booker allows himself to be sucked into a turgid maelstrom of plots and counter-plots leading inexorably (i.e. predictably) to the ultra-suave Secretary of State designate Conrad Morgan (James Franciscus) and a boozily self-flagellating aide with the misleadingly evocative name of Edgar J. Harolds (Dana Andrews).

Peddling an interpretation of the Vietnam period so simplistic as to verge on the tautological, this is the kind of movie where the villains helpfully spell out their villainy on every conceivable pretext (Morgan, rationalizing with cool aplomb the deal he struck with the North Vietnamese: "Expedience built this country. The end justifies the means."), the heroes suffer no more than a fleeting twinge of doubt as they ramrod their way through due process ("Whatever happened to the good old days when John Wayne and Randolph Scott were glad to have their asses shot off for the good old US of A?") and everyone poses the type of ill-phrased question any half-competent scriptwriter would know had to be thrown out ("Are you certain of your intelligence?" Booker hilariously asks the CIA agent who is supplying him with information).

In the Hollywood mentality, Vietnam was inextricably yoked to crime, with war-weary veterans attempting valiantly to 'go straight' but unable to shake off the lingering odor of carnage that attracted criminality to them and often brought about the violent death they had escaped on the battlefield. John Flynn's sleek thriller *Rolling Thunder* (1978) spun a familiar tale of an ex-POW, Major Charles Rane (William Devane), pursuing singlemindedly — and, as we shall see, literally singlehandedly — the killers of his wife and son. But Paul Shrader's characteristically overblown script did manage to add a couple of grisly turns to the screw: what causes the thugs' lethal cupidity is the televised pres-

Converse (foreground) comes under fire.

Ray Hicks (Nick Nolte) and Marge Converse (Tuesday Weld) – ***'DOG SOLDIERS'***

entation to Rane from a grateful home town of a silver dollar for every day of his captivity; and, after his hand has been mashed by a mechanical waste disposal unit (his prison camp ordeal has fortified him against torture and, it is suggested, even given him a taste for it), he sharpens the hook that replaces it into the deadliest of weapons. Otherwise, it was the mixture as before, with the occasional monochrome flashback of Rane suffering at the hands of his VC captors to remind us of what its makers hoped the movie was about.

Oddly enough, *Rolling Thunder* presented one of the few cases of a vet returning to his *wife:* this facet of the question, surely rich

Ray Hicks lies mortally wounded at the end of the road.

Maj. John. T. Booker (Chuck Norris) leads his crack troops – ***'GOOD GUYS WEAR BLACK'***

in dramatic possibilities, was consistently ignored by the cinema of the period. There *was* Mark Robson's *Limbo* (1973), but it dealt more specifically with 'Vietnam widows' (not in the literal but the 'golf widow' sense), the wives of men taken prisoner or missing in action. Perhaps because Robson was an old Hollywood trooper whose first directorial assignments dated from the early 40s, it emerged as the kind of genteel, sometimes touching melodrama (with an antiwar slant) that used to star June Allyson or Teresa Wright. Its denouement, however, a parody of the traditional 'happy ending', was disturbingly effective: the heroine's just released husband returns to a firing squad of TV cameras and a young wife who hardly knows him and never had time to love him, Robson sealing their uncertain reunion with a freeze frame rather than the reassuring 'happy ever after' fade out.

If by 1973 the antiwar position had already acquired an aura of respectability, Hal Ashby demonstrated that five years later, especially in the southern tip of Jerry Brown's lotos state, it was blessed with full Establishment approval. In *Coming Home, the* 'returning vet' movie, a good dose of radical politics suffices to cure the disabled veteran Luke (Jon Voight) of all his mental — and apparently quite a few of his physical — ailments (as if being crippled were somehow a more benign affliction in the balmy spiritual climate of Southern California). Luke, paralyzed from the waist down, is first seen in an overcrowded, none too efficiently run army hospital in Los Angeles, wheeling himself along its constricted corridors on a stretcher bed on which he is obliged to lie face downwards. Though his initial encounter with the movie's heroine, Sally (Jane Fonda), is marked by the kind of realistically squalid grace note that wouldn't have been possible before the 70s — she upsets his urine bag — their mutual involvement is still in the classic novelettish tradition of a wounded soldier's regeneration through the devotion of a beautiful nurse. And one who, coupled with his growing commitment to antiwar activism in the wake of a disturbed fellow patient's suicide, will make a new man of Luke.

Soon he has exchanged his stretcher for a wheelchair which he maneuvers with such ease, speed and mobility that one almost suffers a twinge of envy watching him scoot around. A few football games, a candlelit dinner at Sally's new apartment and his embitterment would seem to have been dissipated, as if all along it had been directed more against his admittedly humiliating confinement to a stretcher than the permanence of his condition and the war that caused it. Luke himself moves back into a well-appointed apartment and retrieves his smart sports car from the garage (but then, as everyone knows, the inhabitants of Southern California are blissfully ignorant of anything so vulgar as financial problems).

Understandably reluctant to slow down while he is ahead, he makes a pass at Sally, whose gentle but firm "I've never been unfaithful to my husband", whether kindly or literally intended, is in the circumstances a rebuff of truly astonishing tact. Or is it — for, in fact, at this point in the proceedings neither she nor the spectator realizes just what she might be missing. When, in protest against his friend's suicide, Luke chains himself to the iron gates of a USMC Recruit Depot (a remarkably tricky operation from the looks of it even for someone in full possession of his physical capacities), Sally, seeing the incident on television, rushes over and proposes to spend the night with him. No sweat: after a few decorous preliminaries in the bathroom, Luke emerges in his wheelchair, his nudity protected by a small towel over his crotch, clambers into bed (without crucially disturbing the towel) and in a series of tasteful dissolves accompanied on the soundtrack by the occasional anxious query — "What should I do now?" or "Can you feel this?" — Sally, not without hang-ups of her own, achieves her first orgasm.

Since the movie never chooses to disclose the precise extent of Luke's physical abilities, the audience must accept his sexual

Maj. Booker deals with a state department agent in customary style.

Kate Jackson, Kathleen Nolan and Katherine Justice meet representatives of the North Vietnamese government – ***'LIMBO'***

prowess on faith. It no longer seems to matter that, in an earlier scene, a crippled black patient has complained to Sally about the dearth of advice offered disabled vets on their future sex lives (a delicate problem which was, however, intelligently handled by a less permissive Hollywood in such movies as William Wyler's *The Best Years of Our Lives,* 1946, and Fred Zinnemann's *The Men,* 1950, in which Marlon Brando played a paraplegic). But *Coming Home,* glossing over these potentially awkward practicalities, opts instead for facile beach-party bucolics, with Luke breezily coasting Sally along on the arm of his wheelchair (as if it were one of the bicycles in *Butch Cassidy)* to the vapid, Mantovani-like strains of Lennon and McCartney's 'Strawberry Fields Forever'. (It should be said that the movie's soundtrack score is one of the most dispensable in the history of the cinema: an ultra-relaxed medley of popular songs from the late 60s, serving neither to underline nor counterpoint the visuals, almost as if Ashby had had a huge jukebox placed on the set in which he remembered, from time to time, to insert a coin).

But the moment has come to focus, via a flashback, on the character of Sally herself. When her Marine captain husband, Bob (Bruce Dern), is shipped out to Vietnam — "Combat City", as he jovially refers to it — she decides to volunteer for unpaid nursing duty in the local veterans hospital. Sally is a model Army spouse: hair stiffly permed and ribboned, make-up unimaginatively applied, skirt worn just above the knees with a neat little matching blouse, she frets about her husband minding that she has taken a job in his absence and stands to attention for the national anthem on TV. Which adds up to a *character role* for Jane Fonda. In view of an average audience's familiarity with the actress's personal appearance and much publicized politics, she will necessarily be perceived at the beginning of the movie as in disguise: a disguise, moreover, that the spectator cannot help mentally 'correcting', to the detriment of any pretence to realism that the movie might harbor.

But her involvement with Luke and affection for the liberated Vi (Penelope Milford), the girlfriend of one of Bob's fellow officers, gradually causes her to loosen up. She takes to wearing teeshirt and jeans, moves out of her house on the base into a cramped apartment overlooking the beach, buys a weird little speedster and, most dramatically, allows her hair to adopt its natural frizz. In short, *she turns into Jane Fonda.* It's possible to measure her disenchantment with the values to which her drab life has hitherto been consecrated by these outward changes in fortune; in fact, it's essential, since precious few more resonant clues are provided (an exception, however, and one of the movie's most sharply observed scenes, is her vain endeavor to interest the ladies of the camp's gossip sheet in publishing a spread on the veterans' plight — one contributor even voices qualms about the propriety of any feminine presence in the wards: " When I was on my diet, I didn't want candy lying about the house").

Resplendent in her new Jane Fonda hairdo, her external aspect coinciding at last with her long repressed inner self, Sally runs into Luke on his first exhilarating excursion by wheelchair. Their mutual euphoria is enshrined in the script's sole (unwitting ?) stab at a rhyming couplet: "You got a chair!" "You changed your hair!" Both have been freed from straitjackets, as it were, and Ashby appears to regard Sally's curls as no less significant an advance than Luke's graduation to semi-vertical mobility. Later, about to

Maj. Charles Rane (William Devane) interrogates a member of the gang who killed his wife and son – ***'ROLLING THUNDER'***

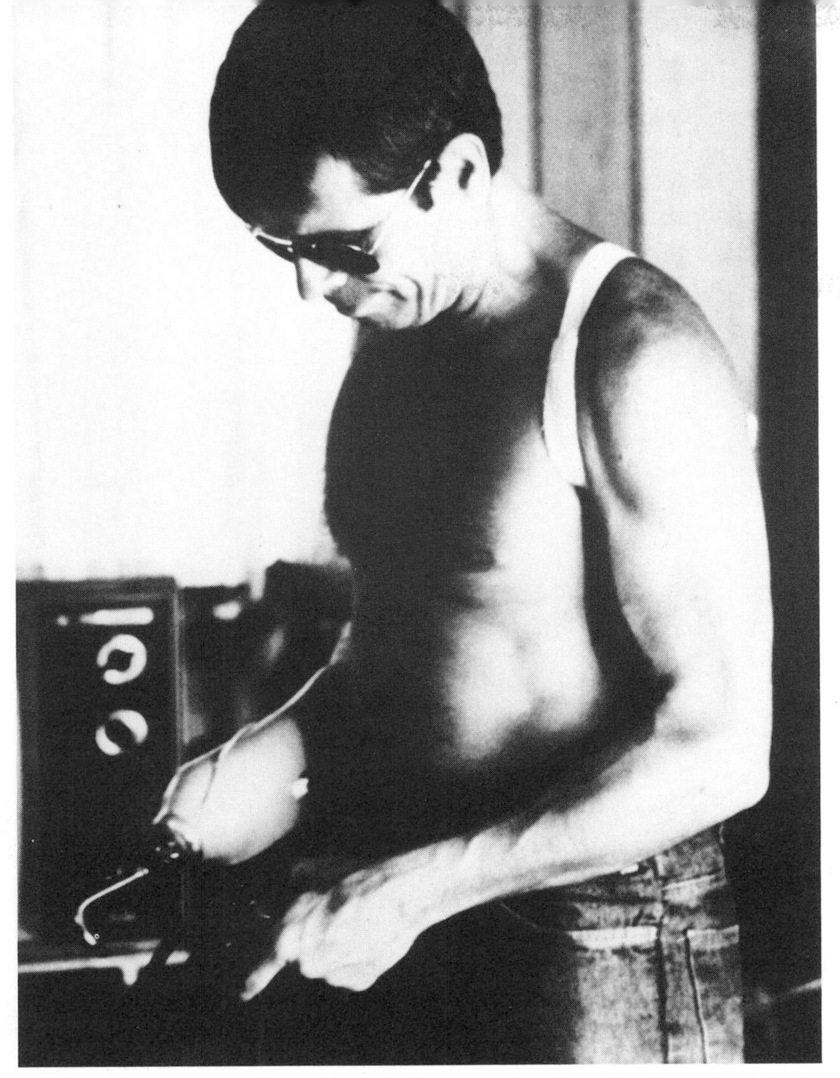

Maj. Rane refamiliarizes himself with the handling of a gun after losing his right hand – ***'ROLLING THUNDER'***

join Bob on leave in Hong Kong, she loyally has her hair restraightened and unearths all those klutzy army wife outfits once so rapturously discarded; but luckily, on her return, sex with Luke will practically make her hair frizz back overnight. Sally, it's clear, has had a narrow escape: had there been no Vietnam, who knows what might have happened to her.

Notwithstanding the movie's emphasis on the Luke-Sally axis, a slightly more subtle characterization is reserved for Bob (an excellent performance by Dern in a thankless role). In the parallel montage with which the movie begins, a cynical discussion between the embittered hospital vets is intercut with shots of Bob jogging in preparation for imminent overseas service. But his whole professional existence has been a preparation for this moment: such a soldier *needs* Vietnam, if only to justify his choice of career. Later, however, he sees things differently. On leave in Hong Kong, he is asked what the war is like. "I don't know what it's like. I only know what it is. TV shows what it's like. It sure as hell don't show what it is." And in the intimacy of their hotel room he struggles to describe to Sally how he discovered his own men cold-bloodedly decapitating corpses and skewering the heads on top of poles. "Y'know, that really scares the shit outa the VC..." he adds in a half-defensive tone that suggests some of the Vietcong's fear has rubbed off on him.

Bob's untimely repatriation is prompted by a minor leg wound that may have been accidental or self-inflicted but for which he has in any case been given a medal, as if it were a poultice. It's one of *Coming Home's* unintentionally comic side-effects, reinforced by the striking contrast between Bob's chronic rigidity of character and Luke's elfin vitality, that his limp emerges as a rather more serious affliction than Luke's only mildly inconvenient paralysis. Since the demonstration at the Recruit Depot, the activities of the two young lovers, racing around the beach community in Luke's sports car (with its cute registration number VET 210), have been monitored by the FBI and are eventually reported to an uncomprehending Bob. Though Luke, to whose other myriad qualities one must now add that of sagacious counsellor, persuades him of Sally's unabated love, Bob pulls off his uniform (and medal) and plunges naked into the ocean (an act widely if prematurely interpreted as his suicide, just as in a Hollywood movie a slight cough will invariably betoken the onset of a fatal disease). Ashby employs a second parallel montage here to intercut Bob's symbolic self-cleansing with Luke spouting antiwar platitudes to local high school kids.

What makes Bob a more complex figure than might be apparent from such an ungenerous resumé is precisely that his psychological make-up rejects the type of glib frog-into-prince metamorphosis that overtakes the others. If Vietnam has significantly altered the lives of Sally and Luke, its influence has been strangely *beneficial* (the latter's disability excepted): Sally has liberated herself from the complacently genteel routine of a dutiful army wife

Luke Martin (Jon Voight) and Sally Hyde (Jane Fonda) find fulfillment – ***'COMING HOME'***

("Why aren't you out on the golf course ?", a blustery Luke snaps at her after their first meeting in the hospital); and Luke (over whose pre-Vietnam past hangs a whiff of mindless Southern Californian hedonism, as evidenced by his sports car and poolside apartment) has, with his involvement in the protest movement, 'gained a new purpose in life'.

But Bob, who most badly stood in need of a 'happening' on the order of Vietnam, has ironically seen it drain his life of purpose (though one conjectures that, on his re-emergence from the ocean, he might transform himself most radically of all, growing a beard and maybe moving in with a health food restauranteur from Carmel). He went off to fight one war and returned from another. And Dern's performance clearly intimates that the precarious gung ho ethos which has hitherto governed the character's life — and which, though dented, continues to support him through the estrangement of his homecoming — is a form of repression too ingrained to be as nonchalantly reversed as Sally letting her hair down, in both the figurative and literal sense. Not least, his presence provides the script with its sole opportunity of alluding to the physical horror of Vietnam, in a movie which otherwise treats the war as if it were a particularly violent game of squash and the enemy as flat and indistinguishable as a wall. (But it's a disconcerting feature of almost all Vietnam cinema — even a documentary like *Winter Soldier* — that the war's 'victims' are generally understood to be maimed or traumatized *American* soldiery and only incidentally the Vietnamese people).

To be fair, *Coming Home's* sincerity is never in question and on occasion fleshed out by the kind of behavioral detail with which Ashby is most at ease: a hospital picnic, with the basketball-playing, guitar-strumming, pot-smoking inmates indifferent to the attempts of a visiting officer to boost their morale, is nicely judged, as is the recreated barracks atmosphere of the crowded wards (even to the traditional accompaniment of a mournful harmonica). But it's a frisbee of a movie, held aloft by sheer weightlessness; it succeeds in smoothing away all the rough edges of the period (*circa* 1968 from the evidence of a Robert Kennedy speech on television) to leave only the pious certitudes of a later decade's positive thinking. In short, a movie to which,

Luke and Sally flying a kite together.

Luke comforts shell shocked Bill (Robert Carradine) – ***'COMING HOME'***

with the possible exception of Luke's honest-to-goodness bag of piss, not even the ladies of the base newspaper could raise any very strenuous objections.

The only other film (except for *The P.O.W.*, 1973) to deal with the readjustment of maimed veterans was *Just a Little Inconvenience* (1977). I have nothing to add to my BFI Monthly Film Bulletin review:

> Since there can hardly be *two* Theodore J. Flickers, one is forced to conclude that the director of this embarrassingly foolish melodrama is none other than the founder of the Premise Theater of satirical improvisation and amiable *auteur* of *The Troublemaker* and *The President's Analyst.* When that little poser has been fully mulled over, however, virtually nothing remains to engage the spectator's intelligence. Although, according to its voice-off narration, *Just a Little Inconvenience* is based on a true story, the almost indecent speed with which a few skiing sessions enable the embittered amputee (James Stacy, who played a similarly afflicted newspaperman in *Posse)* to "snap out of his depression" – as the pressbook rather indelicately phrases it – successfully propose to a pretty young schoolmistress, and absolve his buddy of any guilt in his disablement offers considerable scope for skepticism. All in all, the principal source of visual stimulation is Lee Major's mobile left eyebrow, which contrives to steal every scene from the rest of his face.

Infinitely more thought-provoking was a TV movie made in 1979 by the English-born director David Greene, *Friendly Fire,* which — remarkably for such a late arrival on the scene — succeeded in taking the thematics of Vietnam cinema down several unbeaten paths. Inspired by an authentic case (fidelity to which extended to leaving the characters' names unchanged), it recounted the efforts of an Iowan Catholic family — with the aid of novelist C. D. B. Bryan, on whose book the movie is based — to

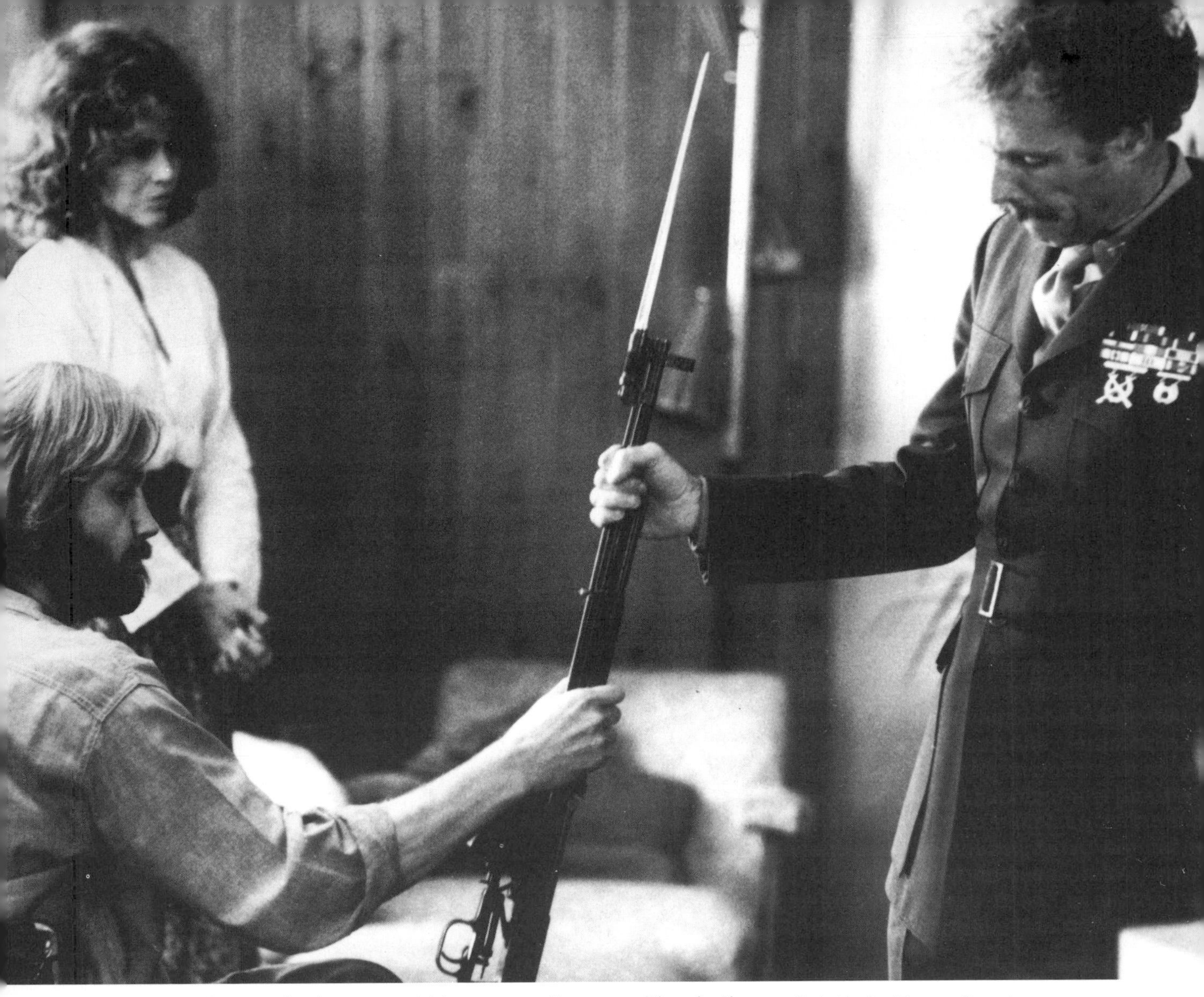

circumvent increasingly paranoid bureaucratic opposition in the form of phonetapping and mail censorship and uncover the truth behind the official version of their son's death in Vietnam. For Sergeant Michael 'Mikey' Mullin (Dennis Erdman) was a victim of the morbidly dubbed 'friendly fire', i.e. fire caused not by enemy action but from the home side, and as such his name was withheld from all the published casualty lists. With the 200 dollars sent them by the army to defray funeral expenses, the Mullins take out a half-page advertisement in the local newspaper urging parents in Iowa to join them in protest against the war, a gesture which results in a bulging mailbag, a nationwide TV appearance and participation in the Washington Peace March.

Bob Hyde (Bruce Dern) decides against violence by handing over his automatic.

So meticulously detailed is its depiction of how issues often deemed to be of 'merely' national concern can with shuddering immediacy be brought home to two bewildered individuals, their initial uncertainties hardening into lonely determination (then, almost imperceptibly, into obsession) that, even with a running time of over two-and-a-half hours, this modestly gripping movie seems hardly a minute too long.

When, for example, the soldier's mother (a bizarrely restrained Carol Burnett) inquires of an attending army officer when her son's body will be flown home, she receives the chilling reply: "Just as soon as they have a planeful"; sent a form letter of commiseration from President Nixon with which is enclosed a dossier of his various speeches on Vietnam, she contemptuously scrawls 'Return to Sender' on the envelope; and confronted at last with Mikey's body in an open casket, she hesitantly confesses that she would have preferred the waxy corpse to be disfigured "... so I could believe he died in a war". No less poignant is the incongruous set of nail file and clippers bought by Mikey's younger sister as a going away present; Mrs Mullen's insistence that her son's tombstone read, not "died in..." but, with blunt literalness, "*killed* in Vietnam"; or the wry observation by a black corporal from Mikey's platoon that the only question ever asked him about his combat experience is "Hey, man, didya kill someone?"

The movie, demonstrating how the war could also transform the *parents* of draftees into social misfits — as Mrs Mullen says of their gradual ostracism by the inhabitants of their home town: "It's like we're on different roads now" — firmly resists the temptation to portray the Mullens as purely altruistic crusaders, untainted by personal considerations. Worrying away compulsively at the conflicting testimonies surrounding Mikey's death, they manage to alienate their immediate family, their oldest friends and finally even Bryan himself (Sam Waterston), whose own involvement with the case meets with less than the full-hearted approval of his wife and his agent. When, after exhaustively interviewing both Mikey's comrades and superiors, Bryan is forced to conclude that his death was indeed an accident, the suspected military coverup being perhaps no more than the jittery reaction of a monolithic organization ill-equipped to deal rationally with such dogged burrowing into its affairs, the Mullens simply don't want to know. It's as if they had been betrayed.

A final title dispassionately informs us that between 1968 and 1973 no fewer than 10,303 American soldiers were known to have died in Vietnam through 'friendly fire'.

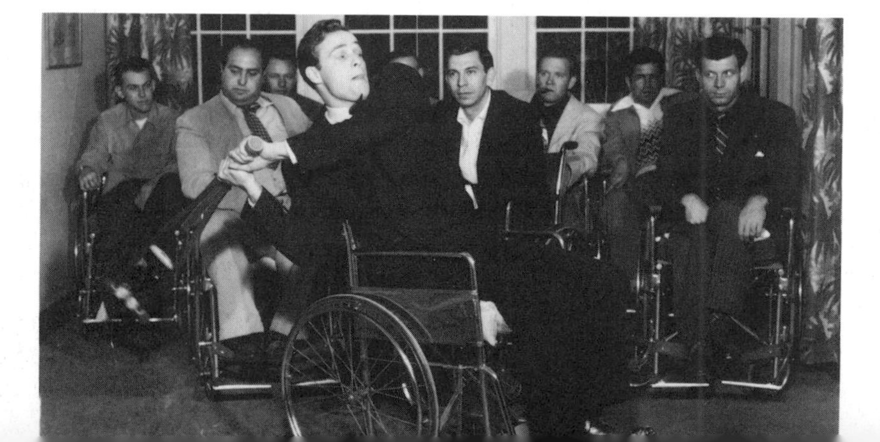

Marlon Brando, as a disabled war vet in Fred Zinnemann's ***'THE MEN'***

SECTION V
GOD BLESS AMERICA

IN THE prologue to *Notes,* a rather scatty memoir of the filming of *Apocalypse Now,* Eleanor Coppola catalogs her husband's efforts by telephone, and frequently via agents, to obtain the services of various Hollywood stars for his upcoming Vietnam movie. McQueen, Brando, Pacino, Caan, Nicholson and Redford all find themselves on the receiving end of these increasingly forlorn calls and, until Brando's agent finally returns one, all either make unacceptable demands (McQueen, offered three million dollars for the seventeen week shooting schedule necessitated by the role of Willard, insists on the same fee to play Kurtz for *three* weeks) or decline outright (Pacino is afraid of tropical diseases, Caan's pregnant wife doesn't want to have her baby in the Philippines, etc.). Eventually (but only after throwing his five Oscars out of the window in frustration), Coppola, as everyone knows, cast Brando as Kurtz and, following the abrupt departure of Harvey Keitel, the then relatively unknown Martin Sheen as Willard.

Hollywood being one vast grapevine, this kind of news would circulate fast. The fact that Coppola, in 1977 a man of thirty-eight but still a boy wonder by the industry's standards, was planning a multi-million dollar epic on the war, though judged in some quarters as a classic instance of a fool rushing in where angels (in the showbiz sense of 'financial backers') had feared to tread, was nevertheless a sign that the subject was at long last coming out of

The soccer match is interrupted – ***'THE BOYS IN COMPANY C'***

quarantine. It would be cynical to attribute the sudden rush of Vietnam movies set into motion after but released before *Apocalypse Now* (Sidney J. Furie's *The Boys in Company C,* produced by the Hong Kong-based company, Golden Harvest, Ted Post's *Go Tell the Spartans* and Michael Cimino's *The Deer Hunter)* less to any urgent moral or political commitment than to the desire to steal the thunder of a movie whose preparatory stages alone had caught Hollywood's imagination — cynical but not necessarily wrong. One shouldn't generalize, of course. While neither *The Boys in Company C* nor *Go Tell the Spartans* is absolutely devoid of interest, they are what one might call 'quickies', if not B movies then resolutely A minus, whose existence seems motivated solely by opportunism. But *The Deer Hunter,* whatever one thinks of it, is a different matter entirely, a long, complex and well-constructed narrative whose inception could not possibly have been inspired by the hope of cashing in on the much-delayed *Apocalypse Now.*

As we have seen, for almost a decade Hollywood had managed to avert its gaze from the horrors of the war itself, opting instead for such Vietnam-related themes as campus unrest and the troubled reintegration of vets into civilian life. For the movie industry Vietnam had been a trauma, a Zeitgeist, a tragic memory, a scar which in time would heal — anything, in short, except a war where people killed and/or got killed. It was evident that, for the 70s, any project bearing even a vague resemblance to *The Green*

Berets was out of the question. Given that the subject-matter was far less charged with the emotive immediacy it had possessed in 1968, certainly no-one would come out in protest — but just as certainly no-one would come out at all. The question was therefore: What should the Vietnam war look like on film? What were the motifs, visual and thematic, that would emerge as dominant, that would reappear in film after film — with greater or lesser variations — to evolve into a codified 'Vietnam style'? Only by formulating a set of genre conventions at the outset, conventions which would be developed, refined or indeed superseded by subsequent movies, could the Hollywood machine come to terms with this still sensitive area.

Neither *The Boys in Company C* nor *Go Tell the Spartans* was to provide a conclusive answer. The former involves a bunch of raw recruits to the US Marine Corps in 1967, with each of whom we become individually acquainted by means of a series of vignettes at the beginning of the movie. Thereafter, we follow them through their basic training, with all its rigors and humiliations, into their tragicomic adventures in combat. Though the purpose of the vignettes (which center on the draftees' arrival at the army base) is primarily to familiarize us with the *dramatis personae* before their identities are subsumed by the merciless leveling process of their training, they can also be taken as a preliminary assertion of the film's somewhat self-conscious pretensions to 'realism'. Not for *The Boys in Company C* the melting-pot sentimentality of those ethnically balanced military units so familiar from World War II movies (or, for that matter, from *The Green Berets:* already on the soundtrack a folksy ballad

Hawkeye and Trapper size up the opposition before the game – ***'M·A·S·H·'***

Burt Reynolds and fellow inmates plan an onfield offensive – ***'THE LONGEST YARD' (G.B. 'MEAN MACHINE')***

"Here I Am" has been substituted for the crudely tub-thumping title theme of the earlier work). For here in effect are Tyrone Washington, a tough black dope peddler (played by *Roots* actor Stan Shaw); Vinnie Fazio, obsessed with sex (Michael Lembeck); Billy Jay Pike, a professional footballer (Andrew Stevens); Dave Bisbee, whose long blond hair and guitar denote the typical counter-culture Jesus (Craig Wasson); and Alvin Forster, an aspiring writer and, like Richard Dreyfuss's Curt in *American Graffiti,* the company's chronicler (James Canning).

But instead of rejecting the old army-as-cross-section-of-humanity cliché, as it patently imagines itself to be doing, this (superficially) heterogeneous collection of individuals merely updates it. Having bracketed three of the recruits respectively with drugs, sex and Flower Power, Furie and his screenwriter Rick Natkin, confident that the movie is now securely plugged into the sacred iconography of the 60s, tend rather arbitrarily to leave it at that. The trouble is that this stratagem puts quite a strain on the characters' psychology. Vinnie, for example, will seldom talk about anything but girls throughout and Dave, despite all that happens to him, will never forfeit his dreamy brand of freakishness. (The footballer's presence, however, is determined solely by the movie's climax in which violent sport is allotted the same dual role as in *M*A*S*H** or Robert Aldrich's *The Longest Yard, GB The Mean Machine:* on the one hand, as a liberating, anti-authoritarian activity; on the other, as 'war in miniature').

Vinnie Fazio (Michael Lembeck) and Alvin Foster (James Canning) are ambushed – ***'THE BOYS IN COMPANY C'***

Threat to authority. Billy Pike (Andrew Stevens) faces up to Capt. Collins (Scott Hylands).

Like some Vietnam recruiting poster beneath whose peeling surface may be glimpsed patches of an earlier one for World War II, the movie cannot disguise the origins of its stereotypes. In the 40s model, some cheap hoodlum of perhaps Sicilian, certainly non-WASP, descent would contrive to earn the grudging esteem of both his buddies and his superiors, just as the black drug pusher does here; the same sexual longings as here would be innocuously channeled into ogling pin-ups of Betty Grable; and the 'writer', represented here by Alvin, would most probably be a 'sensitive' Montgomery Clift type complete with pipe and tattered volume of Hemingway protruding from his kit. And by leaning so heavily on these stereotypes, Furie is obliged to turn recent history on its head: as we know, service in Vietnam was inclined to transform ordinary, basically decent young Americans into misfits, dropouts, drug addicts, petty criminals or whatever — not the reverse. Since Hollywood had already dramatized the kind of situation where vets were treated as outsiders by the very society that had made them so, being denied the automatic respect and respectability to which returning GIs have traditionally been entitled (for a few years, at least), it was surely not too much to expect the first movies dealing directly with the war experience to offer some insights into what exactly had changed. But for *The Boys in Company C* the army, however much it might brutalize its charges, however riddled it might be with corruption and incompetence (the movie's judgement, not mine), somehow remains the institution best fitted to make responsible adults out of confused and callow youths. Here misfits are turned into men, not men into misfits.

Dave Bisbee (Craig Wasson) reunited with his guitar after a V.C. ambush.

Though what one sees of the training period *is* numbingly brutal — and the shrill litany of obscenities accompanying every single command makes it no less hard on the ear — and though the presumably morale-boosting refrain of "We're the biggest, baddest, meanest mother-fuckers in the valley" chanted on every conceivable occasion makes "The Brave Men of the Green Beret" sound positively refreshing in retrospect, when our heroes emerge at the other end, ready for overseas duty, it's as a tight, well-knit fighting unit, the pride and terror of the base. Moreover, the initially surly and uncommunicative black has matured into their natural leader, winning a stripe to prove it. As the harassed captain, enlisting his aid during a man-to-man talk, puts it: "I've got eight weeks to teach these goddam shits what you learned in twenty years on the street" (a confirmation of *Taxi Driver's* thesis that nothing less than guerilla tactics will ensure survival in the ghettos of New York). And what with the company's growing camaraderie, its rough edges honed by exposure to Washington's street-wise skills, a nicer, more regular bunch of soldiers you could never hope to meet.

So after extracting half-an-hour's worth of grisly humor from the routine indignities of Marine Corps training (whose usefulness is brought home to the conscripts by having them stand on parade clutching their most precious and vulnerable possessions: their testicles), *The Boys in Company C* arrives, with the unit's imminent departure for South-East Asia, at precisely the same point that a World War II movie would have taken five minutes to reach. As Dr. Johnson *didn't* say, cynicism is the last resort of the patriot. Here their disillusionment (about the army, *never* about the war) seems to have no real satirical purpose that one can discern. To be sure, tiny tremors of shock are registered *en route* (subject, however, to swiftly diminishing returns) and the tediously unremitting obscenities finally bludgeon one into accepting them as part of the texture of army existence that the movie seeks to illustrate. But the ideological assumptions on which that existence is based are never questioned, nor is the irony of young Americans being brainwashed to prevent a similar fate befalling the Vietnamese.

Only at the thought of Vietnam itself does the characters' cynicism desert them; and their mixture of anticipation and dread over being posted there is neatly suggested by the scene where one of them, failing to recognize a body bag, playfully zips himself into it as if it were for sleeping in. When he learns of its real use, he struggles in superstitious panic to free himself.

Once it gets to Vietnam the movie marginally improves. Its most impressive feature, perhaps, is that the enemy remains unseen, a shadowy, eerily invisible presence hovering just at the edge of the screen. In contrast to more apocalyptic Vietnam movies, *The Boys in Company C* comes close to capturing the feel of guerilla warfare: in the way the Viet Cong, advancing through the undergrowth with a sense of self-camouflage so instinctive that even stealth can be dispensed with, become almost part of the jungle fauna; or in the way they exchange signals that, by a disorienting reversal, imitate parrot cries, forcing the hapless intruders — who were trained as soldiers, not hunters — into a paralyzing state of permanent watchfulness. This approach, making the VC threat a near-abstraction (and therefore untainted by the racist slurs of *The Green Berets* and *The Deer Hunter),* means that the movie's tension arises mainly from conflicts within the army itself and, later, with the ARVN.

Tyrone Washington (Stan Shaw) Lt. Archer (James Whitmore) and Billy Pike in another scene from the soccer stadium.

But whereas the attacks on military obtuseness in the first half-hour were rather scattershot, finding little to criticize beyond foul language and the kind of petty sadism common to all institutions governed by rigid discipline, here they prove more effective because directed against more precise targets. Already Vinnie, for example, incurring the Colonel's wrath by sleeping with his daughter, has had his cushy posting in the Pacific changed to a combat one. In Vietnam the company is assigned to a Capt. Collins (Scott Hylands), an unstable commander whose over-riding concern is with obtaining good 'body counts', no matter the identity of the bodies: he counts indiscriminately VC and peasants, men and women, adults and children. When, after escorting a trailer through enemy-infested terrain to an inland base — and suffering casualties along the way due to Collins' bungling leadership — they discover it to contain, not supplies as they had imagined, but cases of liquor, packs of cigarettes and other luxuries for the General and his cronies, Bisbee protests by blowing it up (apparently at no disciplinary risk to himself). And Pike, tormented by having advised his girlfriend to abort her pregnancy, is plied with drugs by the megalomaniac Collins, who is anxious to exploit his skills on the football field against a crack Vietnamese team.

*Maj. Asa Barker (Burt Lancaster) stands for no insubordination. – **'GO TELL THE SPARTANS'***

Cowboy (Evan Kim) attempts to gain information from a V.C. prisoner – ***'GO TELL THE SPARTANS'***

Since all this in-fighting ends by upstaging the real war, there may be another explanation for the enemy's absence: that, at least by the late 60s, such was the disaffection of the American forces from the cause for which they were ostensibly fighting that the war began to be treated as a nagging annoyance, a *drag,* impinging only temporarily on their life, liberty and pursuit of happiness. More pressing concerns, the movie suggests, were those of health and hygiene: in short, more VD than VC. Only Alvin seems unaffected by the prevailing opportunism: he had genuinely hoped to be posted to the front in order to document the company's experiences; in a Da Nang brothel he confines himself to chatting with the prostitutes, thereby arousing in Vinnie the suspicion that he might be homosexual; and, of course, it is he who gets killed during the final offensive.

Meanwhile Washington, though still the company's mainstay and increasingly its conscience (as exemplified by several huge, soulful close-ups), has formed the idea of smuggling drugs back into the States concealed in the kind of shapeless body bag no customs officer would dream of disturbing. Such a plan, however, would involve the collaboration of the local ARVN security chief, Colonel Trang, who with his chubby, beringed fingers and one elongated fingernail *à la* Fu Manchu bears a striking resemblance to the corrupt *Viet Cong* general of *The Green Berets.* When Washington learns not only that Trang's way with suspects is to torture first *then* give them the third degree but that he's wholly untroubled by misgivings in putting body bags to such use, he withdraws from the scheme in disgust.

One last test will suffice to complete Washington's and the company's education in ethics. Collins informs them that if they beat the local Vietnamese soccer team, they will be removed from active duty and sent on a prestige tour of Japan and other neutral countries of South-East Asia. Even Pike, deeply resentful of the captain's underhand methods, agrees to participate when he hears that he has become a father after all. But at half-time, with the Americans easy winners so far and elated by the prospect of ending their service in such enjoyable fashion, they discover that Trang has insisted on the conditions of the bargain being changed: as a means of boosting Vietnamese morale, the team is now expected to lose the match. Jeered by the spectators — and by a gloating Trang in the seat of honor — as they allow the opposition to run rings around them (literally), they suddenly follow Pike's lead and begin playing to win again, though fully realizing it will mean their return to the combat zone. No sooner has victory been declared, however, than a surprise Viet Cong attack creates havoc in the stadium and claims its first victim in Alvin.

If this sequence has been recounted at some length, it's because it usefully encapsulates the confusion to which the whole movie has been prone. To begin with, certain discrepancies of plot and motivation go unexplained. For example, what precise relation is the movie trying to establish between the advent of fatherhood and playing a soccer match? If a victory for the host team is intended to boost Vietnamese morale, surely the ludicrously obvious way the Americans go about losing — scoring through their own goalposts, protractedly tying boot-laces, etc. — can only be counterproductive and even insulting to the 'victors'? And if the latter are (as they appear to be) such wretched sportsmen that they are actually unaware of being mocked, why should defeating them in the first place have justified sending the Americans on a demonstration tour?

But one would be prepared to forgive such minor flaws if they were not directly traceable to a basic moral ambiguity at the core of the movie. In *The Loneliness of the Long Distance Runner,* Alan Sillitoe hit on an indelible image of revolt with his adolescent athlete who, about to win a race for the greater glory of the reformatory in which he is interned, stops a few yards from the tape and refuses to cross it. Already this gesture was coarsened by the American athletes at the Mexico City Olympics in 1968, when they raised their fists in a Black Panther salute only *after* winning the event and securing their medals; and in *The Boys in Company C* what subversive charge it once possessed is further undermined by its taking the form of a refusal to *lose.* Though the target of the team's defiance is the half-mad Collins (as well as the evil Trang), the audience cannot help but perceive their act as a victory for American *esprit de corps,* as an exhilarating expression of Yankee grace under pressure. So what if they flirt along the way with antisocial, unAmerican behavior — Washington's drug-running scheme, Pike's wish to have his unborn child aborted — in the end, as one would expect of red-blooded American boys, *they come through.* And it's impossible not to feel that since they have opted to remain in Vietnam, by God, 'Charlie' had better look out! Notwithstanding unscrupulous allies and incompetent, even corrupt superiors, this war can hardly be the dishonest fiasco its detractors would make out if it enables Washington, Pike, Bisbee, Vinnie and Alvin to overcome their individual problems and work so well together as a team. Why, it could even be called therapeutic.

But if the movie flunks on all the larger issues, it can at least be credited with usefully exploring some of the incidentals. It has a semi-documentary aspect that isn't negligible. We learn, for example, what body bags look like, what material they are made of, how they zip open. We learn that body counts can be (and often were) artificially jacked up by the inclusion of civilian victims, as confirmed by Peter Brook's theatrical dramatization of Vietnam politics and attitudes, *US* (subsequently recorded on film by Peter Whitehead in *Benefit of the Doubt* and adapted *for* film by Brook himself as *Tell Me Lies,* both 1967). And the dilapidated *USO* base with its improvised bowling alley and "Esther Williams" pool, though as spectacle no match for Coppola's strobe-lit pleasure palace rising out of the jungle in *Apocalypse Now,* is undoubtedly far closer to reality. Even the monotony engendered by the movie's self-indulgent insistence on the Spartan horrors of Marine Corps training, served up in neatly packaged episodes of 'pre-sliced' life, probably does convey an accurate picture of what an average draftee would undergo (as against the archly humorous treatment of draft induction in *Big Wednesday,* whose artful dodgers hope to pass themselves off as cripples or outrageously effeminate homosexuals). These are secondary virtues, perhaps, but authentic ones.

Muc Wa – The French military cemetery from the previous war – ***'GO TELL THE SPARTANS'***

G.I's return fire. Sgt. Oleonowski (Jonathan Goldsmith) – ***'GO TELL THE SPARTANS'***

Go Tell the Spartans is set in 1964, as the French colonial war was coinciding in its final stages with the full and official assumption of Vietnam as an American responsibility (where before the United States had been involved in an ill-defined 'advisory' capacity). Though this has the oddly nostalgic effect of situating the whole *débâcle* even further back in history than, from the viewpoint of 1978, it actually was (an impression reinforced by the fact that two of its principal characters had already fought together in Korea), it works to the extent that it focuses our attention for once on a precise juncture of the war. In general, Hollywood has portrayed Vietnam as a kind of phantasmagoric limbo, untrammeled by dates or place names, all 'middle' with no real, definable beginning or end. Such a vision of the war will recur right through the 70s until apotheosized in *Apocalypse Now.*

The movie's protagonist (played by Burt Lancaster) is Major Asa Barker, a professional soldier and commander of an American Military Assistance Advisory Group at Penang. Barker is a battered also-ran of three wars, whose hopes of promotion beyond the rank of Major were blighted when he was caught by the President and his own general enjoying fellatio with the latter's wife — in the White House. As the movie opens, he has just received the order to scout an unoccupied hamlet called Muc Wa (the title of the original novel by Daniel Ford was *Incident at Muc Wa*); judging it to be of doubtful value, however, he sends in a false report. But when the General insists that Muc Wa's position

Linda (Meryl Streep), Michael (Robert De Niro) and Stephen (John Savage) at the latter's wedding – ***'THE DEER HUNTER'***

on the coastal road to Penang makes it strategically important, Barker reluctantly dispatches a group of new 'advisers' who have been assigned to his command. These are Second Lieutenant Hamilton (Joe Unger), naive, untested, fiercely jingoistic, i.e. a young soldier of the old school; Corporal Courcey (Craig Wasson, a real Vietnam war movie vet — he played Bisbee in *The Boys in Company C*), an intelligent, personable draftee whose presence in Vietnam, at a period when virtually no draftees were posted there, mystifies Barker; the battle-weary and slightly 'punch-drunk' Sergeant Oleonowski (Jonathan Goldsmith), who served under Barker in Korea; and a Corporal Abraham Lincoln (Dennis Howard), whose only resemblance to his namesake would seem to be a perpetually lugubrious mien (probably caused in his case by being so named). Accompanying them is a raggedy complement of South Vietnamese soldiers, peasants (both old and very young) and local mercenaries, led by a bloodthirsty Viet Cong-hater nicknamed 'Cowboy' (Evan Kim).

So, except for the vast difference in stature and temperament between Barker and Capt. Collins (aided by Lancaster's 'star quality'), the basic narrative components are similar to those of *The Boys in Company C,* but the coolly even tone of Post's movie could hardly be further removed from the calculated hysteria of Furie's. Although a sense of disillusionment with both military values and objectives is no less pervasive in *Go Tell the Spartans,* it evolves naturally out of precise, realistic and, on the whole, convincing character developments. Instead of heroes and villians, Them against Us, the movie is crisscrossed by shades of imperfection on both sides. Barker himself is no model soldier (in either sense of the phrase), his intelligence and generosity being apparently the fruits of experience rather than of any innate superiority. When the black signalman Toffee (Hilly Hicks) persists in employing an irreverent form of address — "Hey, Major" — he makes a show of objecting more, one suspects, for

Michael participates in an attack on a V.C. village.

old times sake than out of any faith in military hierarchy. Not that Barker has done anything so pretentious as yield to despair: for him (and this will be the keynote of the whole movie) Vietnam is just another war, his third.

The composition of the unit departs from both the World War II movie cross-section, uniform in its very variety, and the coarsely updated caricatures of *The Boys in Company C.* Its members seem almost *arbitrarily* selected, by which I intend a compliment to the movie. In life, surely, army units would resist such facile division into one good-natured black versus one sadistic white bigot, one lecherous second-generation Italian versus one virginal second-generation Pole, etc. Here the draftee, unlike Wasson's smirking, pot-smoking hippie of the earlier movie, is an attractive, rather reserved and completely *straight* young man who proves quietly expert at his job. The reason he offers Barker for having chosen a posting to Vietnam — that if he had to be a soldier, he wanted to be in "the roughest, toughest unit in the whole US Army" — does make a kind of sense. Though he never claims, like Alvin, to be a 'writer', we feel that the Vietnam experience has been consciously courted, will be stored away and — who knows? — one day put to use. Poor Hamilton, on the other hand, has seen too many movies. Fully intending to pave the jungle of South Vietnam with good intentions, he is a tragi-comic figure whose gestures, purchased secondhand, are fatally ill-adapted to Vietnam combat. About to leave for Muc Wa, he gives his motley crew the standard pep talk, as stale as a sermon, only to see Oleonowski take over and whip up the required fanaticism by screaming "Kill Communists! Kill Communists!"; assigned to measure the increase in mosquito bites when insecticide is not

Michael Cimino directs the same scene.

applied, he bravely bares his own arm, remarking stiffly to Courcey: "I never ask my men to do anything I wouldn't do myself"; and after a skirmish with the VC, he radios back the message: "We have met the enemy and they are ours", causing an incredulous Barker to choke on his coffee. In short, he goes by the film — as one says, by the book.

Only Oleonowski's angst seems pitched too high: his eventual suicide — by retiring into his quarters and putting a pistol to his forehead — is undoubtedly the least plausible event in the movie, because so blatantly derivative, in style if not in substance, of hackneyed, a-man's-gotta-do-what-a-man's-gotta-do heroics.

In general, *Go Tell the Spartans* is a decent, average war movie (surprisingly so from the director of *Good Guys Wear Black)* whose mostly run-of-the-mill qualities become exceptional only in the exceptional context of Vietnam cinema. Its vaguely absurdist attitude to the war prevents it from ever embracing the obscene complacency of *The Green Berets;* and perhaps the highest praise one can pay it is that — while in the movie theater, at least — one seldom questions its unfocused attitude to the political ambiguities of American involvement. Like countless minor Westerns, for example, it gives the impression of drawing on a well-worn set of genre conventions — *except that there is no Vietnam war genre.*

This emerges most powerfully in its treatment of both the Viet Cong and South Vietnamese. On a scouting foray, Courcey encounters a group of displaced peasants, all women, old men and babes in arms. Disregarding Cowboy's vehement protests,

Michael and Stephen imprisoned by the V.C. await their turn at Russian rculette.

Hamilton allows them to shelter in the encampment ("Our task is also to win the hearts and minds of the Vietnamese people"). One pretty young girl takes to dogging Courcey's footsteps.

Barker (who has been helicoptered out to Muc Wa): "Are you screwing her?"

Courcey: "No, sir!"

Barker (wistfully): "Well, somebody ought to... " Later, he is heard to say: "Better pump that little cunt full of penicillin before the whole barracks come down with the clap."

When they are finally ordered to evacuate Muc Wa in the face of a massive Viet Cong build up, Courcey, outraged by the decision to abandon Cowboy and the South Vietnamese, elects to stay behind and Barker, grudgingly impressed by this gesture, joins him. At which point, we discover that Cowboy's hatred of the Viet Cong, even if neurotic in its intensity, hadn't blinded him: his instinct that the group of peasants befriended by Courcey were VC sympathizers is proved right. Even the tiniest tots, caught making their escape in the night and gunned down by the mercenaries, are swathed in ammunition belts. The sole survivor of their massacre is the young girl, who subsequently (a shade

... whilst Nick (Christopher Walken) is forced to play the game by his captors.

predictable, this) attempts to kill Courcey.

Earlier, Barker has resorted to bribing an ARVN Colonel Minh (Clyde Susatsu) to raise artillery and air support for the increasingly beleaguered garrison. Minh's venality is patent enough: the elegant French drawing room, the rather too glamorous interpreter, the cases of cognac guilelessly stacked against the wall, not to mention the unctuous suavity of his own con man style. But this, once again, is held within strictly credible bounds — even erring on the side of modesty when compared to several well-documented scandals involving the South Vietnamese military — and bears little resemblance to the comic strip Oriental heinousness of Colonel Trang in *The Boys in Company C.*

Though the Vietnamese are as usual denied psychological 'equality' with the American characters, they are at least allowed their reasons. Cowboy may deal summarily with prisoners by decapitating them or potential informants by half-drowning them but, given the circumstances of his own death — shot by one of the refugees — his judgment, if not the severity of his methods, is validated. If the VC appear devious in their use of women and children as infiltrators, the uninhabitable devastation around Muc Wa would demonstrate, were no further evidence available, that they have plenty to be devious about. One aged war victim, his features as cracked and rutted as a quarry, hovers ominously on the fringe of the action, slipping unseen into the undergrowth at the approach of a soldier. After the ambush, when the wounded Courcey painfully drags himself to his feet and prepares for the long trek back to Penang, this wizened spectre finally steps forward to point a revolver at him. Courcey, strangely unfazed, just calls out, "I'm goin' home... I'm goin' home..." and hobbles off. Whereupon, the wretched old man apparently expires. The End.

But, throughout, an almost elegiac strain of melancholy underlies the movie's rough-and-tumble surface: it's perceptible in the scene where Lincoln, stoned on opium, scrambles up the watchtower at Muc Wa and proceeds to chant the Gettysburg Address in a sing-song (and oddly 'Vietnamese') voice; in Barker's wry nostalgia for "a real war", one in which he might be "hitting the beach at Anzio", instead of this "sucker's tour, going nowhere, just round and round in circles"; and in the reiterated American rumbles of "It's *their* war... " Most curious, and revealing, in this respect is the emphasis placed by the script on a continuity of defeat between the recent French humiliation and the gruff confidence of the American military command. The determination of this second wave of invaders not to repeat the errors of the first — the French, according to Barker, "got tied down in static defense" — finds its *reductio ad absurdum* when he is upbraided by his superior for referring to his company's 'esprit'. ("That's a French word, isn't it?") At the beginning, the link seems ironically intended; but, little by little, the movie is infused with a kind of romantic fatalism, culminating in the discovery of the French cemetery at Muc Wa. On its wooden portal can be read (from Herodotus' account of the Battle of Thermopylae and the 300 Spartans): "Stranger, when you find us lying here, go tell the Spartans we obeyed their orders."

(Burt Lancaster also starred in Robert Aldrich's *Twilight's Last Gleaming*, 1977, as a deranged ex-Air Force General who threatens to launch nine atomic missiles from a Strategic Air Command silo unless the President accepts to read on nationwide television a secret document pertaining to the escalation of the war. Though, as the following extract from that document will show, Aldrich's analysis of the rationale behind American involvement as an exercise in limited warfare is crude and simplistic, his movie remains virtually unique in having polemically engaged with the issues at all. It reads in part: "...the objective of this war is to demonstrate to the Russians a brutal national will, that we have the willingness to inflict and suffer untold punishment. That no matter what the cost in American blood, we would perpetrate a theatrical holocaust").

More subtly controversial than *The Green Berets* and perhaps more durably so than *Apocalypse Now,* Michael Cimino's *The Deer Hunter* had as checkered a history after it opened as Coppola's movie before. Cimino (who collaborated with *Apocalypse Now* scenarist John Milius on the screenplay of *Magnum Force,* 1973, which was directed by none other than Ted Post of *Go Tell the Spartans* and *Good Guys Wear Black)* had only one previous feature film to his credit, *Thunderbolt and Lightfoot,* (1974), a heist trifle with Clint Eastwood. Given this rather unprepossessing pedigree, the movie's pre-release publicity was much less aggressively pitched than that of *Apocalypse Now,* which meant that the subsequent risk of disappointment was that much less great. In fact, it became an immediate success both commercially and critically, sweeping the board at the 1979 Oscars. But critics writing in specialized magazines proved less adulatory than daily or weekly reviewers, and the existence of a growing backlash was confirmed (in some quarters) at the same year's Berlin Festival,

Michael helps Steven retain his grip on the chopper after their breakout.

where *The Deer Hunter* was the official American entry: judging the movie an affront to the struggles of the Vietnamese people, the Soviet delegation withdrew in protest, followed by the Hungarians, Bulgarians, East Germans, Czechs and Cubans.

The Deer Hunter is a before-and-after ad for the USA. 'Before' is a few days prior to its protagonists' drafting to Vietnam; 'after' recounts the efforts of the strongest among them, Michael (Robert De Niro), to piece together the shattered fragments of their lives; and 'during', the most sensational and violent panel of its triptych form, is the war itself. Which, of course, doesn't automatically make it an advertisement for anything – but that it is I hope to demonstrate in the course of this chapter. In its attempt to wrest from the Vietnam experience a positive or, at least, tolerable statement, it resembles another lengthy movie, William Wyler's *The Best Years of Our Lives* (1946), about three discharged servicemen — from the army, navy and air force — in the immediate aftermath of World War II. Both deal with the psychologically destructive imprint of war on three male friends (even if the postwar period, covered by only one 'act' of *The Deer Hunter,* occupies the whole of *The Best Years of Our Lives);* in both the theme of psychological infirmity is mirrored by that of physical amputation; and both close with a ritualized affirmation of national values emerging (relatively) unscathed from the ordeal.

Yet the divergences are even more revealing. In Wyler's film, the unseen, off-screen war remains an abstraction, its necessity never questioned, its hurts those inflicted by any war, indeed, by War itself. But for Americans the Vietnam war wasn't merely the first real military defeat in their history (notwithstanding Nixon's cant pretence of "peace with honor"), it was their first war — along with Korea, perhaps — which resisted every endeavor to inflate it into War itself. World War I, for example, had been a tragically under-motivated conflict, whose origins could therefore be blandly ascribed to some atavistic urge overcoming humanity every thirty years or so to ravage large areas of the planet: war as global hygiene, helping to reduce population levels and encourage reconstruction. (In any case, the United States had intervened late, mainly in order to extricate its European allies from a debilitating stalemate.) World War II had been a 'just' war and, dispensing this time with the ironic pincers of quotation marks, a necessary one: war as crusade. Both were ghastly but — so the argument ran — inevitable.

It was during Vietnam, however, that the whole glassy concept of 'war with a capital W' lost all credibility, a phenomenon which every movie on the subject (even *The Green Berets)* was obliged to take into account. Cimino's movie, like Wyler's, is concerned with themes of renewal and reconciliation; and even in an era marked by racial violence, ecological warnings, Watergate and the

Vietnam hangover itself, he could still place his faith in the United States to achieve these goals: the final scene finds Michael and his friends singing "God Bless America" together. Only then does Steven (John Savage), whose legs have been amputated, succeed in overcoming his bitterness (whereas in the earlier movie the amputee, Harold Russell, appeared to harbor no resentment whatever at his disability). It's significant, too, that Nick (Christopher Walken) is shot, not in combat, but playing Russian roulette in a Saigon gambling den just before the city falls to the Viet Cong. The point is that Cimino's intentions are basically the same as Wyler's: to restore his audience's confidence in their country's regenerative powers, which took a bad mauling in the 60s; and his intelligence lies in the fact that, by insisting on just how long the tunnel has been, he is able to make the light, when it first glimmers on the horizon, so convincing.

As with the war, the small town to which, in *The Best Years of Our Lives,* Fredric March, Dana Andrews and Russell return, though less sentimentalized than a Saturday Evening Post magazine cover, is hardly less idealized in the iconography of its archetypes. The use of grainy newsreel film stock, for example, during the scene in which the three ex-servicemen rediscover their hometown points up Wyler's intention to universalize his setting,

Grim view for Nick from the Saigon hospital where he recuperates.

to ensure that it will be every spectator's idea, dream or memory of Smalltown, USA. But, with the increasing fragmentation of American society after the convulsions of the 60s, it's now no longer admissible to paint small town existence in purely *symbolic* terms, i.e. with the broad, generalizing brush-strokes employed by Wyler. The Pennsylvanian steelworking community of *The Deer Hunter* is therefore particularized to the point where its inhabitants are mostly of Russian Orthodox extraction. Even so, apart from the fact that the presence of such immigrants from a remote Communist country offers the reverse image of second or third generation American sons (when later, in a Saigon hospital, Nick is asked if his name, Chevotarevich, is Russian, he replies: "No, it's American") being dispatched to another, equally remote country which Communists threaten to overrun, Cimino cunningly devotes the first hour-long section of the movie to one of the codified celebrations of American-ness, a white wedding — precisely the ritual that ends *The Best Years of Our Lives.*

Here, in short, is a close-up of that America which Michael, Nick and Steven have been called upon to 'defend', and it would be churlish not to admit that Cimino has recreated the textures of a small, tightly knit industrial community with an almost novelistic wealth of detail: the local supermarket where Nick's girlfriend Linda (Meryl Streep) works, the masculine clutter of the bungalow shared by Nick and Michael, the dark silhouette, both ominous and reassuring, of the iron foundry, and the entanglement of TV aerials and bulbous church domes peacefully cohabiting the town's skyline. This part of the movie is bathed in the Edenic atmosphere of a huge, extended and classless family (as rarely in the American cinema, one has the impression of everyone knowing everyone else), felt most strongly during the wedding party itself, a spectacular setpiece of dancing — both Russian heel-dance and American rock — singing, eating and drinking, with neatly laundered children, plump Slavic grannies

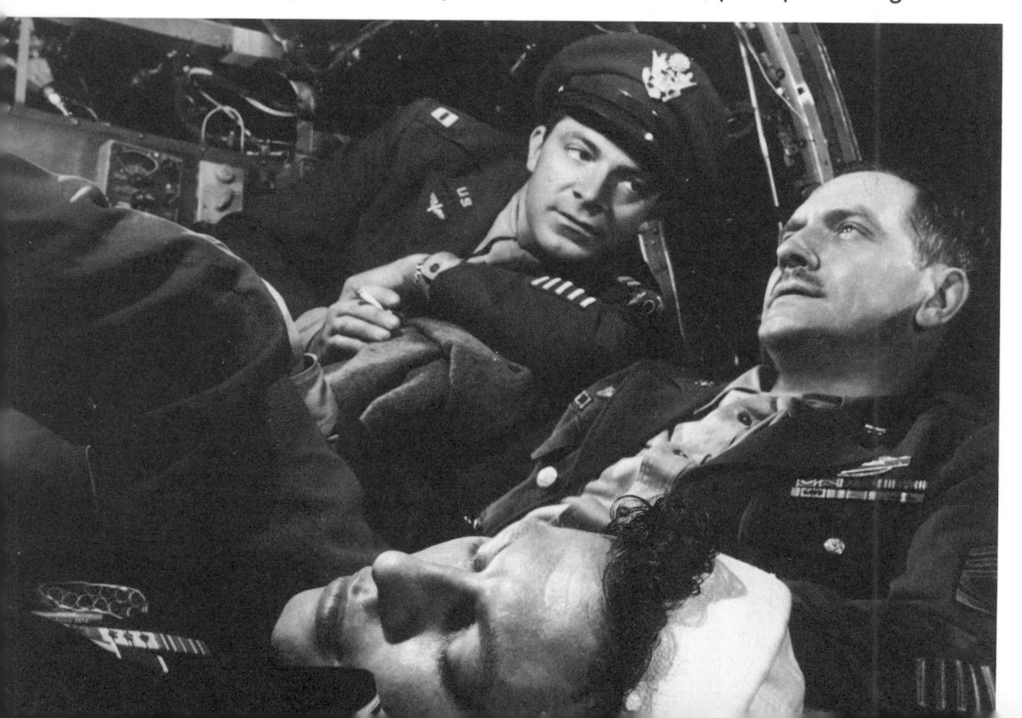

Homer Parish (Harold Russell) foreground, Fred Derry (Dana Andrews left and Al Stephenson (Frederic March) return home in William Wyler's ***'THE BEST YEARS OF OUR LIVES'***

and garrulous old American Legionnaires packing every corner of the screen. What makes the sequence so effective — given that the spectator has paid to see a movie publicized as being about the war — is that, by dwelling at such length on what is unashamedly a glorification of traditional values, Cimino so completely distracts our attention from the approaching nightmare that when, like the movie's protagonists, we are abruptly transported to Vietnam, the contrast with what has gone before is genuinely shocking.

However, two minor but disturbing occurrences cast a shadow over the proceedings. When, in accordance with the Russian custom, the newlyweds, Steven and Angela (Rutanya Alda), link arms and drink from each other's goblets during the ceremony, one fateful droplet of red wine spills (unnoticed) onto Angela's gown. And later, at the height of the revelry, a solitary Green Beret walks into the bar. When toasted by the jocular, slightly tipsy soldiers-to-be and offered a drink, he sourly declines even to acknowledge their gesture of complicity.

After the wedding, that reaffirmation of community oneness, comes a ritual re-enactment of male superiority: the hunt. The hunting party comprises Michael, Nick, Stan, a morosely insecure womanizer and the butt of the group's jokes (played by John Cazale, a fine actor who died shortly after completing the movie), John, the proprietor of the bar (George Dzundza), and the heavyset and monosyllabic Axel (played by a nonprofessional, Chuck Aspegren), the latter three not bound for Vietnam. Michael himself is the Deer Hunter, dedicated and deadly serious (he refuses on principle to lend his spare pair of boots to Stan), for whom hunting is also, and perhaps primarily, a somewhat mystical communion with nature. This is Hemingway country, with civilized man purifying in the wilderness a soul grown soft and flabby (and if the 'wilderness' happens to be located just a few miles out of town, this too is in keeping with the self-deluding novelist). It's also Fenimore Cooper frontier country (and Cooper's best-known novel was, of course, entitled *The Deerslayer)* , 'frontier' signifying anywhere a man cares to make it, anywhere he can practise the frontiersman virtues of independence, self-reliance and an ease with weapons which are kept as well-greased as racehorses. It's also, alas, Marlboro country, shot in a way that it could advertise some hypervirile brand of cigarettes. The choir heard on the soundtrack, for example, as Michael and Nick reach the cold, clean air of the mountains is not a 'heavenly' one (it reprises the church music of the wedding) but Cimino employs it to the same uplifting effect.

Between the beery, extrovert spontaneity of the celebration and the tight, claustrophobic framing of the Vietnam sequences, this scene exudes a Bambi-like innocence. The allusion is less frivolous than might at first be supposed: Disney's *Bambi* was a seminal movie for more than one generation of American children, in whom the death of Bambi's father and his own ascension to leadership of the pack must have tapped quite a few deep-seated, not to say Oedipal, emotions. And it also illuminates one of the scene's (and the whole movie's) more sinister traits: its Fascism, latent here but consciously assumed in the Vietnam section. When the critic Jonathan Rosenbaum wrote of "The intense pantheism and towering vistas of the film's landscape shots, the poetic innocence and purity of the heroine, the telepathy and empathy shown by animals (...), the sheer terror of her flight from angry villagers and the sheer intolerance of their persecution, the misty idealism of the blue light shining on a mountain top before it is despoiled by greedy invaders", he was not describing *Bambi* but *The Blue Light,* a German film directed in 1932 by Leni Riefenstahl, subsequently the cinema's chronicler of Nazism (and reputedly Hitler's mistress), in whose work he detected a strong parallel with Disney. Like Riefenstahl's, *The Deer Hunter's* mountain landscapes are, so to speak, 'white', 'Aryan', a distillation of elemental purity, both natural and, by a subconscious extension, racial.

Even the killing that must take place is 'pure', a contest of equally matched wills between hunter and hunted. 'Equally matched' because Michael kills deer with a single bullet. This, the movie's pivotal metaphor, to be developed through the Russian roulette scenes, is unquestionably linked to the historical ideology of Fascism: killing as an elitist, almost Godlike rite, legitimized by a spurious affinity with gladiatorial combat, medieval tournaments and the duelling scars sported by Prussian cavalrymen as proudly as if they were medals. It seeks to invest

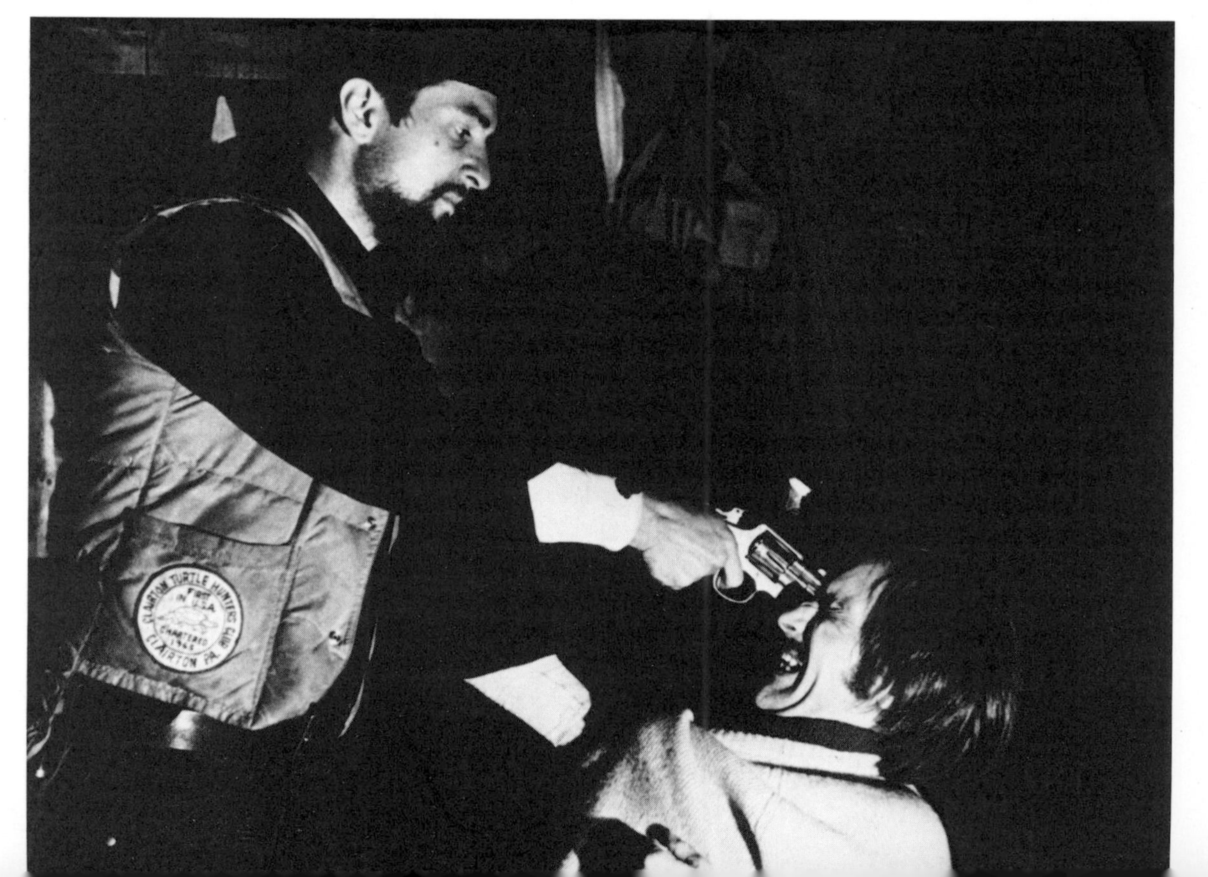

Michael proves a point to Stan (John Cazale) – ***'THE DEER HUNTER'***

killing with the lonely nobility of suicide, another act requiring no more than one bullet.

Later, on their return, they spend a tranquil moment drinking in John's bar. Overhead, a propellor fan lazily revolves. Suddenly on its rhythmic flap-flap-flap is superimposed a deeper, ominously familiar whirring. Cut. A US Army helicopter surveys a fire attack on a Vietnamese village. Michael is seen wielding a flame thrower as expertly as if it were a blowtorch in the iron foundry. A Viet Cong raises a bamboo shelter beneath which cower a huddle of peasants, mostly women and children: he tosses a grenade inside and closes the shelter. Michael, Nick and Steven are captured by the VC and imprisoned in a bamboo cage which is submerged in a rat- and corpse-infested river under a pontoon shack. At which point, the movie turns its back on the war altogether (except for a few incidental images of refugees streaming along a road and, toward the end, the fall of Saigon) to focus on the dual spaces of cage and shack, in which another deadly but now unequal contest is played out between captors and captives.

The Viet Cong unceremoniously drag their American and ARVN prisoners out of the river and force them to play Russian roulette while they themselves lay bets on their chances of survival. Now, given the pitch of tension maintained by Cimino throughout (a tension generated as much by his faster cutting and use of close-ups as by the material itself), there is no way this sequence can fail to make an impact on the spectator. The undiluted savagery of the VC tormentors, the slaps they administer to any victim unwilling or unable to pull the trigger on himself, the ear-grating clicks when a chamber is empty and earsplitting explosions when it is not, the extraordinarily well-controlled hysteria of the performances (Walken, in particular, who in the earlier scenes seemed an improbably orchidaceous creature to have strayed so far from Park Avenue) — all these factors contribute to creating suspense as visceral as one has ever experienced in the American cinema.

But, however skillfully realized, this is still a clear case of manipulating the audience. So forceful is the imagery in its own right that we are bereft of those critical faculties which might, with a less accomplished movie, contest the depictions of the Viet Cong (and in *The Deer Hunter* they are all the Vietnamese we see) as sadistic tyrants whose gambling mania, an undeniable phenomenon of life in South-East Asia, has found its ultimate gratification in playing with human dice. Yet, since the movie is not a documentary, why should we worry at its cavalier treatment of recent historical fact? When questioned, Cimino, shamefacedly acknowledging that he had never heard of such a game being played during the war, pleaded dramatic license. His was a movie about America, not Vietnam, about how the war changed — and, by changing, strengthened — America's appreciation of its most deeply ingrained traditions, most notably that of individualism within equality; and if these themes emerged most vividly through a misrepresentation of facts, he was, he believed, justified in using it. What complicates one's response is that the invention functions so effectively, both in its literal enactment and as a metaphor not only for the obscene logic of war itself — where a man's death may result from his being, as fortuitously as a bullet, in the wrong place at the right time — but also, via Michael's dedication to clean killing, for the whole frontiersman myth and its uneasy but still potent application to the twentieth century.

Thus, though *The Deer Hunter* articulates no overtly political discourse, though like his protagonists Cimino never for a moment questions why *he* is in Vietnam, he does indirectly raise a fundamental issue: How far should an artist be free to deform the 'truth' in the pursuit of avowedly aesthetic aims? The problem is especially thorny where Vietnam is concerned, as the crude racism and political obfuscation of many World War II movies, even if not considered instruments of propaganda, were founded on a consensus of Amercan, Western and, indeed, almost global opinion. The Japs and the Krauts *were* the bad guys. As such, they deserved to be held up to the good guys' scorn. Already highly debatable, this argument becomes untenable when no consensus exists, as with the Vietnam war, or when the consensus has shifted, as over the years with the nation's treatment of its Indian population. In the latter case, a number of movies were made in this period portraying the Indians as the victims of land grabbing rapacity (e.g. *Soldier Blue,* Arthur Penn's *Little Big Man,* 1970, both of which were also viewed as parables of Vietnam) or else, enshrined in a framework of almost religious iconography, as doomed 'noble savages' (Dolores Del Rio's Madonna of the wigwams in Ford's solemnly elegiac *Cheyenne Autumn,* 1964). But these works, eschewing the myth-making rhetoric of the best-loved traditional Westerns, only confirmed that Hollywood's chronic tendency to mythologize everything it touched had rendered it incapable of dealing conceptually with major historical currents.

The Deer Hunter however, is set firmly in the 'classic' mold. Which means that in order to inflate its hero to mythic stature — for Michael, when divested both of the actor's charismatic presence and the character's romantic huntsman trappings, is after all a blue collar steelworker whose beliefs include the sanctity of marriage (Stan hints at the possibility that he might be a virgin) and, presumably, opposition to any form of gun control legislation — it is obliged to dehumanize the enemy. The question is therefore not whether Cimino has taken liberties with documented fact (which is, by definition, the prerogative of any work of fiction) but whether his distortions represent an adequate response to the factual background that his movie exploits. Here the failure is total. Whereas in Eisenstein's masterpiece about the Russian Revolution, *October* (1927), the gross caricatures of gross capitalists possessed their own crude vitality — one might say, they leapt off the screen — Cimino's Viet Cong cannot even be called one-dimensional. They exist merely to objectify Occidental fears of the yellow race. Their addiction to Russian roulette serves no discernible purpose beyond their own titillation and profit: no valuable information, for example, is being forcibly elicited from their country's enemies. In a straightforward guts 'n' glory movie, with both sides reduced to the cardboard cutout dimensions of archetypal hero and villain, such characterizations would still be reprehensible; here, given the (intended) psychological depth of the American characters as well as the enormously detailed canvas of their environment, they constitute an insult not only to the 'heroic struggles of the Vietnamese people' but to the audience's intelligence.

It's through Michael's steely presence of mind that the trio of friends eventually manage to make their escape. He persuades his bemused captors to grant him first one, then two extra bullets in the revolver, thereby suicidally raising the odds against his own survival. But the ploy succeeds: the randomly chosen chamber proves empty and with his accumulation of bullets he instantly guns down the VC. Michael and Nick release Steven (but apparently none of his fellow prisoners) from the bamboo cage and they begin to float downriver. They are sighted by a US Army helicopter. Though Nick is picked up, Michael and Steven lose their grip on its runners and once more plunge into the river, Steven breaking both his legs on a submerged ridge of rocks.

'The Deer Hunter'. Michael back in the mountains in search of his quarry.

Michael subsequently hauls Steven through the jungle and onto the pretentiously but poignantly named Interstate 9 where, in spite of the fleeing peasantry, he finds him a refuge on the bonnet of an ARVN jeep. Second-act curtain.

The final section properly belongs to Michael — his return to Pennsylvania, his deepening affection for Linda and his efforts to force the embittered Steven into a reconciliation with Angela — but it's perhaps Nick's story that holds most interest from the point of view of this study. Still numbed by his ordeal, he cannot bring himself to call Linda from a public phone booth in the American Military Hospital in Saigon. He wanders aimlessly into the city's congested streets which the movie depicts (these scenes were shot in Thailand) as an inferno of massage parlors and garish clip joints. In one of them, the Mississippi Saloon, decked out with wagon wheels and go-go dancers, he accepts the advances of a prostitute but reneges when he discovers a baby in the squalor of her tiny room. Further on, he notices bodies being surreptitiously ferried through a somber alleyway and suddenly finds himself drawn into a dimly lit house where two young Vietnamese with scarlet headbands are voluntarily playing Russian roulette (a short-term engagement, one gathers) amid a crowd of frenzied gamblers. On an impulse Nick seizes the pistol from a startled player and fires an empty chamber into his own forehead. Later, as the city is about to fall, Michael, after much greasing of palms, will himself be led into that same smoky caepharnum to confront a drugged, heavy-lidded Nick, wearing a red headband as a sign of his professional status.

Nick has, in short, 'gone native', with all the lurid implications hinted at in colonialist usage of the phrase. For Cimino's Vietnam is only a slightly updated version of that poisonous Oriental lotos land of ineffable pleasures and pains that Hollywood in the 30s (e.g. Josef von Sternberg's *Shanghai Express,* 1932, with Marlene Dietrich) would construct on its backlot like a jigsaw puzzle: a world of prostitutes suspended in cages, waterfronts veiled by fishing nets, the swish of softly beaded doorways, coolie-infested shelves of opium dens, and mandarinesque conversations that seemed to be conducted entirely in fortune cookie proverbs... And when Julien, the somewhat ambiguous French entrepreneur who has lured Nick into the gaming house, extracts a bottle of champagne and two long-stemmed glasses from the back seat of his elegant coupé, the last piece has fallen into place.

Vietnam is a hell on earth, but was not made so — the film seems to suggest — by the American presence. If American involvement was wrong-headed and even criminal, it was only because it exposed 'our boys' to contamination by a continent so irredeemably mired in moral corruption and the debilitating lethe induced by opium that it hardly deserved to be saved. The unspoken question hanging over the movie would seem to be less "Why are we Vietnam?" than "How can the President allow our soldiers to be contaminated by gooks?" For it's contamination by an insidiously demoralizing civilization that causes Nick's death — as, with Michael saying "I love you" to him across the gaming table and a hint of recognition flickering in his eyes, his luck finally runs out and a bullet with his name on it finds its way into the chamber. And, if less directly, it's contamination that makes Steven only 'half a man'. To Michael is left the Herculean task of binding the wounds and reconciling the survivors to an uncertain but hopeful future: he brings Nick home to be buried, he consummates his love for Linda, he reunites Steven with his young wife. But even he has been infected: returning to the mountains, he finds himself unable to kill the deer he has sighted, almost as if killing for him has been *sullied* by contact with an unworthy prey. "Okay!" he shouts, perched high on a precipice beside a waterfall, in a florid shot that might have served as an ad for *giving up* Marlboro cigarettes.

After Nick's funeral, Michael, Steven, Angela, Linda, Stan, Axel and John gather in the latter's bar for a wake breakfast of scrambled eggs and coffee. Rendered inarticulate with grief, they raise their glasses to Nick's memory and slowly, haltingly, both moved and embarrassed, break into a rendition of 'God Bless America'. In many respects, an extraordinarily audacious moment, this, both impressive in its sheer nerve and dispiriting in its recourse to such a trumpery, impersonal expression of feeling for the movie's closing image. The naive patriotism of the hymn's lyrics would seem to rule out the possibility of its being used without irony. But, as with military marches, rational objections to the content of patriotic anthems seem to formulate themselves on one level of our consciousness, while on another, at once deeper and more shallow, one which we have never quite succeeded in deconditioning, we reluctantly yield to their dubious but affecting sentiments. So Cimino has it both ways, exploiting the sentimental jingoism of 'God Bless America' at the same time as he undermines it, just as Furie tried to do with the football match that ends *The Boys in Company C.* Even if we don't 'believe' it, even if we refuse to submit to what we can plainly see is emotional bullying, some part of us wishes it all were true.

The need to shape fiction, or myth, out of our collective experience is as old as awareness itself. Even the pretension to 'telling the truth' about a political reality, be it Vietnam, the Russian Revolution or the American Civil War, becomes part of the myth-making process, since the notion that there can be one indivisible truth about any event is itself a myth (albeit a long dying one). If film-makers subject the framing of their material to a process of creative sifting and selection, so too do journalists; and since the political Zeitgeist can never be reduced to a mere cluster of facts, fiction-makers arguably do the better job of reflecting it. In the 50s, for example, ludicrously low-budget horror movies about beasts from 20,000 fathoms were frequently more sensitive to nuclear paranoia than a heavily loaded message film like Stanley Kramer's *On the Beach,* with all its big guns pointed in the wrong direction. Such movies as *The Green Berets* and *The Deer Hunter* should perhaps be seen less as *about* the Vietnam war, in which capacity their inadequacies are painfully evident, than *part* of it — part, at least, of how it was perceived by Americans — and any history of the period omitting them from its data will necessarily be incomplete.

From this angle, Cimino's movie may be the richest mine of what one might rather indelicately term Vietnamiana. Its attempts to reaffirm the viability of a heroic posture in an unheroic age, revivify the frontier myth when it was being most vigorously contested and, above all, salve the nation's uneasy conscience make it a prime exhibit in any dossier of American attitudes to the war. At the same time, however, a movie should be more than the servile barometer of its audience's aspirations. For social historians, the ideological subtext of, say *The Green Berets* may well prove as worthy of study as that of *The Deer Hunter,* even if the latter is much the stronger work; what is required *now* for the generation that fought or lived through Vietnam, is a movie to challenge our perceptions instead of reinforcing them, dismantle our prejudices instead of indulging them. In this *The Deer Hunter's* failure appears all the more dismaying, as the undoubted breadth of its narrative ambition held out hopes that it might be matched in depth of vision.

But no. God Bless America (and to hell with Vietnam).

Nick's funeral. Michael tosses a single flower onto the coffin. Linda, Stan and Steven – now a paraplegic – look on.

SECTION VI
FULL FRONTAL

AS WE have seen, the uncharacteristic restraint shown by Hollywood in its treatment of the war during the late 60s and early 70s — which is to say, concurrently with both the escalation of hostilities and that of the campus protest movement — derived in part from its awareness that straight media coverage was daily pre-empting the cinema's power to shock. Whereas Francis Coppola's *Apocalypse Now,* touted even before it opened as the 'definitive' Vietnam movie, a legend even *before* its lifetime, had become, when it finally emerged in 1979, almost the memorial to a period willed into hazy oblivion by the vast majority of Americans. In 1976, when shooting began, the national mood was favorable to reconciliation. Passions were cooling, the immediate past was being left to historians. The destitution of Nixon, last and most flagrantly mendacious of all the war's architects, had been followed — via Ford's 'regency' — by the election of Carter, whose principal qualification for the presidency was the wholly negative virtue of having held no previous office in Washington. He was therefore unsullied by either Vietnam or Watergate, those terrible twins of American criminality in which domestic and international aggressions were inextricably interwoven.

But the war had left scars that could not be healed by the bland, ritualized upheavals of party politics. A sentiment of unease persisted, which was subtly and perfidiously exploited by Cimino in *The Deer Hunter.* When the disgraced Nixon was driven from

'Apocalypse Then'. The four figures of doom from the 1921 movie ***'FOUR HORSEMEN OF THE APOCALYPSE'***

the White House, his obstinate refusal to utter a single phrase of genuinely felt contrition denied the nation of what would have been, at least, the relative satisfaction of justice being seen to be done. As if to confirm LBJ's celebrated crack that he could not pee and chew gum at the same time, Nixon's successor (and sometime Vice-President), Gerald Ford, balked at pardoning both his mentor *and* the half million young men whose crime was to have refused to kill. So the draft dodgers were left out in the cold, while Ford opted to save America from the supposedly greater trauma of bringing a now almost universally vilified ex-President to trial for a miscellany of offenses, the worst — though not always the most notorious — of which were those perpetrated on the peoples of South-East Asia. Even as late as 1978 when Carter cautiously proposed a rehabilitation scheme for draft dodgers, it met with widespread apathy and mistrust. If the war had been waged absent-heartedly without songs or slogans (which throughout remained the exclusive prerogative of the campus rebels) and with a growing apprehension that this time 'we' were the enemy, its aftermath was hardly less demoralized.

As Coppola, his wife, his children, housekeeper, baby-sitter, personal projectionist, actors and technicians from his maverick San Francisco-based company, American Zoetrope, flew into Manila for what would turn out to be 238 days of location shooting in the Philippines, no recipes had been established, no procedures laid down on how to make a Vietnam movie in and for the 70s.

In an interview, Coppola described *Apocalypse Now* as "a film experience that would give its audience a sense of the horror, the madness, the sensuousness, and the moral dilemma of the Vietnam war". From the start, however, the moral dilemma was also, to some extent, Coppola's own. The first three 'senses', authenticated by the testimonies of numerous vets, had been vividly evoked in *Dispatches,* a brilliant collection of Vietnam reportages by Michael Herr (whom Coppola subsequently hired to write the voice-off narration of his movie). Although *Apocalypse Now* adapted none of the episodes that figure in the book, its Bosch-like vision of the war was unquestionably colored by the surreal intensity — as if caught under stroboscopic lighting — of Herr's descriptions of jungle combat. To recreate on film what Herr had achieved in print, however, obviously required a great deal of money. Though budgeted originally at 12 to 14 million dollars, *Apocalypse Now* finally cost upward of 31 million, much of that coming out of Coppola's own pocket or from funding for which he, an independent producer retaining ownership of his film, could be held personally accountable. Expensive war movies had been made before, of course, notably Darryl Zanuck's epic of the Normandy Landings, *The Longest Day* (1962). But that had celebrated an Allied victory, one which precipitated the end of World War II. Even Pearl Harbor, the theme of Richard Fleischer's *Tora! Tora! Tora!* (1970), had been a premeditated aggression on a still neutral country — "a date which will live in infamy" in Roosevelt's words — and the film managed to end with a concession to American dignity, the Japanese admiral declaring lugubriously that he had "woken a sleeping giant and filled him with resolve".

The Indochina war, however, was an incontrovertible defeat for the United States, a defeat rendered all the more poisonous by the hindsight realization that its advent had been written on the wall (often literally) as early as LBJ's 'abdication' in 1968 and that hostilities had been prolonged for principally electoral reasons. How then could a spectacular movie be made out of that defeat which would mobilize the public in sufficient numbers to recoup a colossal investment? It's safe to speculate, his politics notwithstanding, that even John Milius had excluded gung ho heroics from his original 1969 screenplay (much modified since by Coppola himself). The vast resources of American firepower had been outmaneuvered by the Viet Cong's guerilla tactics, fueled by a fanaticism born of their sense of fighting for a just cause. After the Calley trial and similar revelations, the image of the GI as a folk-hero had been irretrievably tarnished. Film-makers could not even dodge the main issue by resorting to the dramatization of isolated victories, individual acts of daredevilry plucked from the morass of terror and mindless sadism. These no doubt occurred, but they had never caught the national imagination.

To the liberal way of thinking, American soldiers had been *at best* the innocent bystanders of a technological Armageddon, comparable to the Vietnamese women, old men and children of popular-press mythology. No director would have dared glorify — in the manner of that trio of movies about the Israeli raid on Entebbe Airport — the loony *Mayaguez* incident of 1975, however much applauded by Congress. Therefore, like Cimino's exploitation of the war as a backdrop to a peculiarly 60s variant of 'grace under stress', Coppola's Vietnam epic had to be about *something else,* as well. And this something else could hardly relate to such moral concerns as heroism, compassion, human dignity, all familiar features of traditional war movies.

The structure of *Apocalypse Now* is that of a quest: the quest of one Captain Benjamin Willard (Martin Sheen) for the renegade Green Beret Colonel Walter E. Kurtz (Marlon Brando), who is waging his own private war from a Cambodian temple near the frontier with Vietnam. Before Willard confronts his prey at the end of the film, he will, in true picaresque fashion, meet with a succession of adventures, enshrined by Coppola in a half dozen of the cinema's most mesmerizing set-pieces.

Col. Kilgore (Robert Duvall) trigger-happy warmonger – ***'APOCALYPSE NOW'***

The theme of the Quest can be traced to the very sources of world literature and is frequently overlaid with intimations of religious or mythological mysticism, such as are to be found in all tales centering on the Knights of the Round Table. *Apocalypse Now,* however, has perhaps closer affinities with comic strip or adventure movie paraphrases of the Arthurian legends, where the quest is usually reduced in dimension to the pursuit of some evil, 'fallen knight', invariably Black. Within the extraordinarily limpid, almost hieroglyphic framework of his plotline, Coppola consciously manipulates these and other narrative archetypes, even if they are most effective when most deeply submerged in the verbal and visual textures of the movie. Thus the classified mission to root out and destroy Kurtz is treated as a solemn pact, a covenant sealed between Willard and two tersely laconic army officers at a (round) table laid for lunch. A third character (whose anonymity precisely *identifies* him as a CIA man) speaks only once: to advise Willard that Kurtz's career must be terminated, in the arresting phrase, "with extreme prejudice". The general, offering Willard some shrimp, remarks — in a parody of the ritual test of strength submitted to by any epic hero before he embarks on a perilous enterprise — that if he eats it he will never have to prove his bravery any other way. Then chillingly reminds him that "the mission does not exist nor will it ever exist".

The extremely cramped and claustrophobic framing of this sequence, set in a small room at Nha Trang base, not only increases our sense of the war being waged by remote control, by a concentration of power so unlimited as to be almost abstract, it also hints at a view of modern warfare as an extreme form of organized crime: the military as Mafia. (It was the fabulous box-office returns of *The Godfathers* I and II that guaranteed for Coppola the economic autonomy necessary for a project as grandiose as *Apocalypse Now.)* Willard is a hired assassin, an "errand boy" in Kurtz's words, being briefed for his latest job. And, hundreds of miles up the Nung river, Kurtz is to be made an offer that even he cannot refuse.

Just as his protagonist is no knight in shining armor (we learn that he has already been employed on covert missions for the CIA), so Coppola, like Brecht in *Arturo Ui* equating the rise of Nazism with the convulsive power grabs of Chicago gangsterdom, portrays the manners and methods of the military-industrial complex responsible for Vietnam as identical to those of the Cosa Nostra. The cool, civilized room, its table laid decorously with cold cuts, seems as remote from the nightmarish reality of the war as the spacious mansions of the Mafiosi 'brass' with their amoeba-shaped pools and impeccably trimmed lawns from the rain-swept sidewalks and vacant lots where their orders are carried out, those angst-ridden cityscapes immortalized by *films noirs.* Only the shrimp mockingly foreshadows what is to come. But already in the preceding scene (into which the 70mm version of the movie plunges us without the stabilizing benefit of credit titles), with Willard emerging from an alcoholic stupor in a hotel room in downtown Saigon, the two dissimilar if related sensibilities of mythical quest fiction and hardboiled thriller are edgily reconciled. In a hypnotic series of images slowly dissolving into each other, dreams, memories and hallucinations commingle freely inside Willard's head. A forest landscape, straight out of a painting by Max Ernst, is crisscrossed by helicopters, whose almost invisible presence is signaled by the whir of their rotor blades (one of the emblematic sounds of Vietnam movies, cf. *The Deer Hunter),* like the flapping wings of huge malevolent birds. As Jim Morrison reedily croons "This is the end..." (the first words pronounced in the movie), the forest is suddenly engulfed by flames, as if from a dragon's mouth, and the chop-chopping of blades dissolves into that of a ceiling fan casting its shadow over the prostrate Willard. In this sequence, Vietnam is *literally* what it will become figuratively in the rest of the movie: less a precise geographical (or geopolitical) area than a phantasmagoric landscape etched on the inner eye, an underworld in both the Godfather and God-the-Father sense.

Willard's hotel room is a mess. Its overflowing ashtrays, empty beer cans and rumpled sheets suggest the squalid, vaguely pornographic clutter of some down at the heel private detective, a Sam Spade or Philip Marlowe. (Coincidentally, in the Joseph Conrad novella *Heart of Darkness* which was the direct literary source for Coppola and Milius' scenario, the equivalent of Sheen's character is named Marlow.) This kinship with 40s thrillers is reinforced by the laconically Bogartian vernacular of Herr's first-person narration and the fact that, when a pair of MPs arrive to accompany Willard to the briefing, he groggily inquires what the charges are. Though he is, to his knowledge, innocent of any 'illegal' offense, he has inherited such a legacy of amorality that he hardly knows whether he is due for a medal or a court-martial. When the whole war is a crime, how do you define a 'war crime'? Even his sporadic endeavors to keep himself fit between missions, like Travis Bickle's in *Taxi Driver,* spiral into a paroxysm of violence when he smashes his fist into a mirror (an improvised moment, apparently, with Sheen taking the production crew by surprise and inflicting on himself injuries which Willard will suffer from during part of the film).

If, from its opening shots, *Apocalypse Now* reveals the influence of thrillers and fantasies, Samurai films and even Westerns, one genre to which it bears little resemblance is the traditional war movie. Coppola eschews the realistic, quasi-documentary approach of Raoul Walsh's *Objective Burma* (1945, actually screened to GIs during training sessions) or Samuel Fuller's *Merrill's Marauders* (1961), movies which, though close to newsreels in their depiction of the realities of jungle warfare, nevertheless implicitly endorsed American superiority, physical,

'Get It Right' indeed. Errol Flynn lectures his men in Raoul Walsh's ***'OBJECTIVE BURMA'***

moral and racial. (In the case of Walsh's film, it should be added that its documentary accuracy was puchased at the price of wider historical accuracy: no mention was made of the British role in Burma, of Slim or Wingate.) But Coppola, as we have seen, was denied the assurance of that superiority.

Several commentators on the movie have pointed out that, unlike *The Deer Hunter* with its almost novelistic 'density', there are no real characters in *Apocalypse Now.* Kurtz is a concentration of pure charisma, an aura incarnate and, as the principal bearer of the movie's ideology, a somewhat platitudinous oracle; as a psychologically motivated character, he proves woefully inadequate and not a little risible. With his Cavalry Stetson and canary-colored dickie, Kilgore (Robert Duvall) resembles a David Levine caricature, all top-heavy head perched on a stocky little body, and owes a great deal to Sterling Hayden's paranoid General Jack D. Ripper in Kubrick's *Dr. Strangelove.* And Willard, basically, is a pair of eyes. In fact, Martin Sheen's eyes, on whose dilated pupils the whole eerie slipstream of Vietnam seems to drift past, form the movie's most powerful visual motif, one that is extended to all the minor characters: the patrol boat crew, the bronzed surfers who comprise Kilgore's entourage and the leaderless, half-crazed soldiers shelling an unseen enemy at Do Lung bridge. The war is such a disorienting spectacle that even the most disillusioned 'grunts' — like spectators in a movie theater — constantly stop to register amazement and horror at it. When, at the height of the attack on the coastal village, Kilgore asks the young surfing champion for his impression, he replies that he finds it "very exciting". As it happens, Kilgore was referring specifically to the surf, but the implications are clear. Vietnam is a show, the greatest on earth, a mammoth Disneyland with real crocodiles in the Jungle Cruise, real ghosts in the Haunted House. And *Apocalypse Now* is a guided tour of its scariest 'rides'.

If no World War II movie ever showed its protagonist transfixed in sheer incredulity at the carnage around him, it was mostly because he was just too busy making the world safe for democracy. But it was also that in Vietnam, caught between the monstrous technology of his own side's military machine and an equally faceless enemy at ease in the treacherously swampy terrain and malarial climate, the average American soldier had become an anachronism. Only madmen could hope to survive in this war: ostensibly 'sane' madmen like the three wise monkeys at Willard's briefing session or a more overtly 'mad' madman like Kilgore, who seems to survive through unswerving faith in his own indestructability. But even in madness there has to be method and a kind of restraint: Kurtz, possessing neither, will be eliminated.

Allied troops hit the beach – ***'THE LONGEST DAY'***

As a depiction of "the horror, the madness, the sensuousness" of war, amplified by the visceral you-are-there sensation of its huge 70mm screen tableaux and Dolby Sound (and even more unsettling, perhaps, is what might be termed Dolby Silence, capturing the thousand pinpoints of sound that make up silence in the jungle), *Apocalypse Now* will be hard to surpass. In this light, it might be worth examining in greater detail the movie's most celebrated *morceau de bravoure:* Kilgore's air raid on the village. Solely in terms of spectacle, this sequence has no parallel in any previous war movie. A lot of its fascination, of course, can be (and has been) attributed to the exceptional financial resources at the director's disposal. But, both in shooting and editing, Coppola has organized the material with incomparable brio, from the first images of the phalanx of helicopters (whose low-flying formation has an oddly science-fiction feel) emerging out of a pellucid sky to the final, extraordinary moment when Kilgore attempts to collect his thoughts about the end of the war, before stepping simply and almost with dignity offscreen.

Certain critics, however, even if they admitted to being dazzled by the purely visual pyrotechnics of the scene, accused Coppola of indirectly glorifying what he had presumably intended to indict. The spectator, they would argue, cannot fail to identify with Kilgore's gleeful bloodlust, particularly during the first-person-style shooting (in both senses of the word) of the young Vietnamese woman who, after managing to plant a bomb in the helicopter carrying off an injured American soldier, is sprayed with machine-gun fire.

Although it would be foolish to generalize from any mixed assortment of reactions to a movie, there seems to be a confusion here between two distinct notions: 'exaltation' and 'exultation'. The helicopter attack is undeniably an exalting experience for the spectator. In this, it differs little from such other cinematic set-pieces as the Odessa Steps massacre in Eisenstein's *Battleship Potemkin* (1925) and the shower murder in Hitchcock's *Psycho* (1960) — both, incidentally, sequences of extreme violence. But exultation? To be sure, few of us are unaffected by what the French critic André Bazin called 'the Nero complex', the vicarious pleasure afforded by the representation of large-scale destruction (as witness the success of the disaster movie genre). But what kind of spectator finds himself *exulting* in the devastation of a defenseless village (given that he will make an emotive connection between this purely fictional reconstruction and what he knows to have been a frequent occurrence in the war)? The unrepentant hawk, perhaps. But for anyone politically sympathetic to the Vietnamese cause to feel such uncomplicated exhilaration, he would have to be totally insensitive to the ideological signals that the movie is clearly emitting (not least in the portrait of Kilgore), as well as deaf to the factual information no less clearly conveyed by the dialogue.

Land and sea assault on a V.C. village – ***'APOCALYPSE NOW'***

Item: The village itself, though 'belonging' to the VC, is presented as going peacefully about its business. Indeed, since all we see of it prior to the raid is a neat little schoolhouse from which an orderly column of immaculately dressed children is being led to safety (with, inevitably, a last-minute rescue of the tiniest of all), Coppola might even be criticized for special pleading. *Item:* The decision to bomb this particular community stems from Kilgore's obscenely whimsical desire to watch Lance, the young surfer, ride the waves at the height of the battle. *Item:* Though doubtless a contributing factor to the spectator's own pleasure, 'The Ride of the Valkyries', turned up full blast to "scare the shit out of the slopes", has nevertheless been stripped of all but its most blatantly bellicose, even Nazi connotations — questionable as music criticism, maybe, but an unambiguous (if facile) statement of the movie's intentions.

When it's all over, when the green, purple and yellow smoke clouds have cleared from the beach and the water explosions have ceased, Kilgore takes a deep breath and comments wistfully, "I love the smell of napalm in the morning." The gratification in wholesale slaughter is Kilgore's and his alone — the motto on his helicopter reads "Death From Above". If the movie has encouraged the spectator momentarily to empathize with his brand of sadism, it has also forced him at the same time to draw back, to observe, judge and redefine this sadism through Willard's eyes and his reflection that "If that's how Kilgore fought the war, I began to wonder what they really had against Kurtz." In basing his own shooting style on Kilgore's hideously 'heroic' vision of the operation, complete with bugler romantically framed against the dawn and stereophonically stirring background music, Coppola tries to show how a nineteenth century frontier expansionist program — already made possible, however, by the trampling underfoot of blacks, Indians and Mexican-Americans — has hardened into a self-sustaining power structure, solely bent on suppressing liberty and promoting empire. One is again reminded of Ford and Kissinger, in a notorious photograph, *exulting* over what they patently imagined to be the Teddy Roosevelt-like blood-and-thunder of the Mayaguez adventure. Although the sequence (like the whole movie, like every other movie made about the war) never begins to question why the Americans were in Vietnam, it goes a little way to suggesting, through the specifically cinematic device of spectator identification, why they behaved as they did when they got there.

The character of Kilgore (and Robert Duvall's bold thumbnail sketch of paranoia at ease with itself is far and away the movie's best performance) embodies an inverted Catch-22 situation peculiar to Vietnam: To wage such a war in such a fashion, one would have to be mad. But since this madness appears to assure one a greater chance of survival, perhaps it isn't so mad after all. In some respects, as Willard grudgingly admits, Kilgore proves a 'good' commander. His relationship with his 'boys' is one of affection, a paternalistically protective affection which may be said to verge on homosexuality; in the scene of the beach-party barbecue, with Kilgore softly strumming on a guitar, the movie clearly hints at the fraternal homosexuality of all exclusively male groups and, by extension, of war itself. Even when he virtually orders the reluctant Lance to surf in waters that are still 'hairy' (i.e. under bombardment), he somehow contrives to guarantee his safety and, indeed, Lance does return safe and sound. Kilgore is visibly fighting the wrong war. He might well have emerged from World War II a much-loved, much-decorated maverick in the MacArthur style.

In Vietnam, however, where medals have become an inflationary currency (cf. the one received by Bruce Dern in *Coming Home*), where individual acts of courage are debased by the disparity of military means deployed by the two sides and, in the light of the Calley trial, the phrase 'beyond the call of duty' has acquired a new and sinister significance, his flamboyant gestures and almost mindless disregard of personal security seem disproportionate at best and dangerous at worst. Interestingly, Coppola does credit Kilgore with a certain showy dignity while carefully exposing its limitations and self-aggrandizing nature. In the process of bombing them into the Stone Age, he calls the Vietnamese "fucking savages", but this is admittedly when the helicopter carrying a wounded American soldier is sabotaged; he generously offers water from his canteen to a dying VC, only to lose interest in him when he discovers the presence of the surfing champion. If the consciously John Wayne stance and postures belong to an old frontiersman tradition, one for which even liberals have had a soft spot, Kilgore fails to realize (like Wayne himself in both *The Green Berets* and his hawkish public position on the war) that the context has radically and irrevocably changed.

In a way, Coppola's movie makes better sense of the title *Heart of Darkness* than Conrad's novella. Here the 'darkness' is visited on Vietnam (contrary to *The Deer Hunter's* racist implication that it predated the American invasion), not only by Kilgore's helicopters and two dozen gunships blasting a peaceful hamlet sky-high but also by the cynical and disenchanted Willard, who "couldn't remember how many people he had killed". Vietnam

Clean (Larry Fishburne) and Lance (Sam Bottoms) eagerly await the playmates arrival.

The chopper arrives at the supply depot to an expectant crowd.

(the war rather than the country) is no more than the heart of that darkness, an endless psychodrama, half Theater of Cruelty, half Theater of the Absurd, in which impulses normally lurking just below or intermittently bursting through the crust of civilization are given free rein. (For Occidentals the Orient has always played this cathartic role, from Barrie's *The Admirable Crichton* to Golding's *Lord of the Flies).* And Kurtz's Cambodian enclave was doubtless intended to symbolize the very heart of the heart, the inner sanctum of America's collective unconscious.

Since the whole of *Apocalypse Now* is set in Vietnam, without any external reference point of comparison, the spectator is faced with a world from which every trace of genuine civilization has been mercilessly expunged and replaced by its grotesque parody. One of the movie's most pervasive themes is of colonialism as the reverse side of isolationism: the colonialist (or neocolonialist) never truly leaves home, he takes his home with him, duplicating its values, styles and artefacts wherever he settles. So the South-East Asia of *Apocalypse Now* is also a vision of America: the whole Kilgore set-up, the California-style surfing and beach barbecue, the disc-jockeys on Saigon radio and the enormous, incandescent supply depot, whose apparition in the middle of an equatorial forest is reminiscent of the spacecraft descending at the end of Steven Spielberg's science-fiction movie, *Close Encounters of the Third Kind* (only now *we* are the Martians).

It is there ,while waiting to be refueled, that Willard and the boat crew attend a USO show on a floodlit outdoor stage. Three Playboy Bunnies effectively if somewhat charmlessly bump and grind until the audience of GIs erupts in a frenzy of sexual frustration and the MC, Bill Graham, rushed his charges like scared rabbits back into their helicopter. The real obscenity of this sequence derives less from the mechanically lascivious gestures of the performers (who might be considered the army's cheer-leaders) than from the surreal juxtaposition of American-as-apple-pie razzmatazz and the horror that we know is stalking just outside the compound. Framed by the shifting penumbra of the jungle, the alien culture is revealed in all its preternatural crassness and vulgarity. Nothing could more forcefully explode the hypocritically 'permissive' ideology represented by Hugh Hefner's 'untouchable' puppets than to see them dangled provocatively in front of a mob of sex-hungry GIs, then yanked back at the slightest threat of action. And the whole garish construction of the base recalls one's first glimpse of Las Vegas as its shimmering spires loom out of the Nevada Desert like some neon-lit mirage.

By the same token, Graham strewing smoke bombs onto the stage to fend off a too appreciative public is a minor but telling detail that indicates the degree to which, in this version of Vietnam, the twin technologies (and mythologies) of war and show business overlap and feed upon each other. Another such example is Coppola's own brief cameo as a television director, yelling at the soldiers on the beach to continue fighting without looking at the camera. Even straight TV coverage ends up by fictionalizing the event it is filming. Kilgore shaped a persona from bits and pieces of old John Ford Westerns, and newsreels must serve up a war that looks authentic: i.e. that resembles World War II movies. Maybe if just one of those dazed, haggard faces were to confront the camera directly, staring right into the TV viewer's eyes, a human contact would be established which would make the distancing of the war that much more difficult; the reassuring sense of it's being waged by 'others', with 'our boys' hardly less anonymous than the enemy, would instantly be undermined. Just as American soldiers were able to fight (and also commit the kind of atrocity typified by My Lai) because they had been programmed to think of the enemy as subhuman gooks, so most Americans at home rapidly learnt to live with TV's unrelenting bombardment of Vietnam news by programming themselves to think of their own army as gooks — 'good' gooks, perhaps, but basically strangers, other people's sons, husbands or brothers.

The link with show business is occasionally more tenuous and not systematically used to make an immediate point. Its purpose is rather to enrich the movie's textures, with the spectral, circussy attractiveness of certain decors (the fairy-lit Do Lung bridge, for

Playmate of the year (Cyndi Wood) astride chopper during U.S.O. Show.

example) serving to point up the hallucinatory horror of the narrative. What is interesting, moreover, is that these thematic parallels have not been autocratically imposed on the material from outside, as an extended private joke on Coppola's part. They are most frequently projected by the protagonists themselves, as if they hoped thus to disguise their own inadequacies beneath a more traditional iconography of war. The idea of playing Wagner during the raid on the village is not Coppola's, as it were, but Kilgore's. It doesn't blast out from the movie's soundtrack as much as from a helicopter's loudspeaker system. And if its ostensible aim is to terrify the enemy, it doubtless also provides Kilgore with a suitable audio-visual ambience for his posturing heroics. Later, Dennis Hopper as a photojournalist at Kurtz's court, a freakish relic of the early 60s high on the odor of carnage, will be seen swathed in camera equipment like a guerilla rigged with rifles and hand-grenades.

Conversely, there is the extraordinary scene when, during a lull in the voyage upriver, one of the crew members, the ex-saucier Chef, decides on impulse to gather some mangoes from the

The Montagnard Warriors
'APOCALYPSE NOW'

jungle. Willard accompanies him and together they proceed almost casually through the snarled undergrowth. Suddenly, Willard freezes. The spectator expects a VC patrol; but it's a tiger that silently springs at them from out of the shadows. The startling, slightly comical terror displayed by Chef reminds one of the gag of two small children calmly absorbing all the heterogeneous, multi-channelled violence offered nightly on TV — gangsters mowing each other down, Western gunfights, war movie bombings — only to recoil in terror from a Disney cartoon of the Big Bad Wolf. Though the intensity of Chef's reaction suggests the release of an accumulation of pent-up fear, it can also be attributed to the atavistic and even symbolic (cf. the common anti-American gibe of 'paper tiger') nature of the danger facing him, against which the only defenses he can call on are purely instinctive ones. So he screams and runs. Fear of the war itself, of its consequences to life and limb, is always present, but anesthetized by its very persistence into a dull, throbbing ache, no less for those in the thick of it than for those watching it on their TV screens. (Note, for example, that when the same Chef asks one of Kilgore's pilots why he is sitting on his helmet, the laconic response is that he doesn't want his balls blown off. While snickering incredulously, Chef's immediate reflex is nevertheless to insert his helmet under his crotch).

Just before the boat arrives at the Cambodian frontier, it encounters a sampan which, against the wishes of Willard, the taciturn black captain decides to stop and have checked over. As Chef is cursorily overturning barrels and bursting open food-sacks, a young Vietnamese woman makes an ill-timed movement in the direction of a suspect-looking basket, causing the jittery crew to rake the craft and its occupants with machine-gun fire. Although, judged as a super-production set-piece, this sequence is small in scale and therefore 'disappointing', its value is precisely in that, for the first time in the movie, we are granted a close look at the 'enemy', at those anxious, delicate faces painfully familiar from TV and newspaper coverage of the war. In Kilgore's raid, the village was there only to be annihilated, its existence as an autonomous human community being preceded by its essence, from the American point of view, as a target. With no more than a brief long-shot of the schoolroom prior to the attack, the possibility of spectator identification, however fleeting, was thwarted.

Here, however, we have an opportunity to reconstruct the tragic continuity between those inoffensive peasants and their bloodspattered corpses strewn across the deck only a few seconds later. For the duration of this sequence, the perspective of the movie shifts from the global to the mundane; briefly relaxing his visionary ambitions, Coppola settles for the more modest — if also more affecting — dimensions of a newsreel reportage But its aftermath once more reveals his incapacity to deal with the beleaguered Vietnamese on any level but the most tritely melodramatic. As with the row of doll-like children glimpsed just before the helicopters move in, he fatally loads his argument. The basket toward which the young woman gestured turns out to contain not firearms but ... a puppy dog! Perhaps Coppola felt it wasn't enough to show the pointless massacre of one small group of civilians, that the terrible irony of the confrontation had to be rhetorically inflated till it became a paradigm of the futility of all wars, calculated to draw tears from Curtis LeMay himself. What could better illustrate 'man's inhumanity to man', one imagines him thinking, than a puppy only a few days old? Though the scene possesses the sharp immediacy of a news item, this detail contrives to situate it firmly in the kind of press for which, as an old newspaperman's crack puts it, there's nothing like an animal for giving a story human interest. Whatever the standpoint, therefore, Cimino's reactionary cynicism or Coppola's liberal sentimentality, any consideration of the Vietnamese as fully realized characters remains subservient to their classified ethnic status as 'aliens'.

This weakness mars even his treatment of 'aliens', so to speak, closer to home. Two of the crew members are black: the rather gruff captain, Chief Phillips, and a wild, good-natured kid nicknamed Clean, who spends most of the trip languorously swaying to rock music from his radio. It's in the depiction of their deaths, when approaching Kurtz's hideout, that Coppola's uncertainty of tone is most evident. Clean is the first to go, shot

Francis Ford Coppola directs the warriors in the same scene.

during a VC attack from the river bank. When Phillips discovers his inert body, he lifts him up and tenderly cradles him in his arms. What may be interpreted as the natural and understandable expression of his grief is, however, transformed by lighting and framing into a maudlin Pietà of racial oneness and brotherly solidarity, investing the scene with a significance totally absent from the subsequent murder of Chef. Through his death, Clean becomes almost a symbol for the wrongs committed by America's white establishment against blacks, Indians and, by extension, the Vietnamese themselves.

Phillips' own death proves even more bizarre. As the boat nears the temple stronghold it is bombarded with little blunt sticks by the Montagnard warriors under Kurtz's command (impersonated by members of a tribe of Ifugao Indians). This scene, one of the few to survive intact from Conrad's story, gains extra irony in view of the overwhelmingly technological nature of the war as waged by the Americans (and which is foregrounded in *Apocalypse Now* as in no other Vietnam movie). When the barrage turns lethal, it is surely not fortuitous that the one person killed — skewered by a

Willard (Martin Sheen) sits on the super structure, Lance in the gun cupola, soon after their arrival at Kurtz's temple stronghold.

Willard's reaction of disbelief and consternation on seeing Krutz's stronghold for the first time.

spear — is the black captain. For whether or not consciously intended by Coppola, there *is* a subtle whiff of racism in the decision to have a character of African ancestry fall victim to a weapon more familiar from conventional jungle adventure movies, as if some link of primitiveness were being forged between these two non-American peoples. (In Tay Garnett's *Prestige,* a 1932 drama about the French in Indo-China, suave Adolphe Menjou arrives at an island garrison after a long and arduous journey upriver. When asked by his host if anything untoward occurred, he mentions "a spot of bother with some crocodiles" but adds wittily, "Fortunately, they prefer darker meat." In essence, it appears they still do).

If this seems fanciful, consider the whole concept of Kurtz reigning, like some existential Tarzan, over an army of 'natives' who worship him in authentic 'Great White Master' style. Or the fact that, when Willard finally assassinates Kurtz and reappears on the temple steps, these same tribesmen shuffle aside in awe to clear a passage for him. Or even that, in a version ultimately rejected by Coppola, the film was to have ended with Willard taking Kurtz's place as their idol. Already in 1899, when Conrad wrote *Heart of Darkness,* Kurtz's brand of one-man imperialism was out of date; here, it must appear as grotesquely irrelevant to a movie with claims to portray, in its director's phrase, "the moral dilemma of the Vietnam war".

The journalist (Dennis Hopper), a throwback to the 60s, at the court of King Kurtz.

The Do Lung bridge, described in the haunted voice of an unseen GI as "the asshole of the world" (an idiomatic rewording of 'heart of darkness'?), not only divides Vietnam from Cambodia, it marks the frontier between the surreal, crepuscular but still recognizably real world of the war and a truly Dantesque no-man's-land into which the boat is sucked on a headlong voyage, whose completion will test the very foundations of Willard's by now tenuous grasp on reality. Cambodia, we feel, is beyond everything.

Throughout the trip, Willard has been thoughtfully poring over a voluminous dossier on Kurtz: third-generation soldier, graduated from West Point top of his class, became a Green Beret at 38, etc. At the briefing session, he listened to a recording of Kurtz's voice, musing about a snail crawling over the edge of a razor. Studying press cuttings, photographs and letters, both official and intimate, he becomes increasingly fascinated by this man he has not met but who is drawing him inexorably along the river which he compares to "a main current plugged straight into Kurtz". Never in the history of the cinema, in fact, has a movie so mercilessly protracted the introductory build-up to its leading character (true in so far as Brando was the biggest name in the cast). For almost two hours of running time, the spectator is half-consciously preparing himself for his appearance.

There is a story by the Argentinian fabulist Jorge Luis Borges in which a young Indian student, fallen among outcasts, becomes gradually aware of some higher serenity in their manner, a glow of barely concealed exaltation that could not conceivably emanate from their own flawed souls. He judges it to be the pale reflection of an infinitely greater, saint-like being whom he determines to reach by tracking this glow to its source, a process analogous to that, in Hide-the-Thimble, of 'getting warm'. Which is, with obvious differences, the basic construction of *Apocalypse Now;* a crucial difference being, of course, that for Borges the godlike guru could remain a purely verbal conceit, his existence, if any, wholly contingent on whatever the reader's imagination cared to make of it, whereas Coppola's plot clearly required that Kurtz be visualized. Although the undoubted fascination exerted by Kurtz is, paradoxically, far more tangible during Willard's journey up river than when he himself finally makes an appearance, the question concerning us here is not why this should be so — Brando's understandable inability to make much of the role, the bathetically portentous dialogue (or rather, monologue), the crude religious symbolism — but what on earth Coppola intended him to represent.

Willard goes to confront Kurtz, as the journalist and the sergeant look on aghast.

Willard and Kurtz (Marlon Brando) discuss philosophy in the dark depths of Kurtz's temple.

If he is to be considered the vehicle of the film's ideology, the implications are disturbing, to say the least. When he opines, for example, that the Viet Cong are stronger because more evil, he would seem to be presenting the military's case for American involvement in the war as well as its failure to bring it to a swift and satisfactory conclusion, even if his argument is embodied in a philosophical (or pseudo-philosophical) rather than political discourse. "What is said to be ruthless is very often clarity." Hmmm. Adolf Hitler's sentiments exactly. Coppola strives manfully to keep his mouthpiece (if such he is) on the side of the angels: what is necessary is "on the side of good, the primordial instinct to kill without fear, without reason, without judgment". But the notion of an outfit of mindless thugs killing in a worthy cause is simply too far-fetched to merit serious consideration: someone somewhere has to use a modicum of reason and judgment, and a little healthy fear is often a spur to wisdom.

The inspiration for Kurtz's grisly reflections turns out to be an atrocity once witnessed by him, when the VC entered one of their own communities and lopped off the arms of children who had been inoculated by the Americans. As with Cimino's wholly fictitious attribution to the Vietnamese of a mania for Russian roulette, there is no record of such an incident (whose details recall the equally unfounded rumors of German rapine in Belgium which circulated during World War I) ever having occurred in Vietnam. That it was fabricated for cheap dramatic purposes is depressing enough; even more so is that, prior to Kurtz's appearance, the movie, though it certainly heightened and colored the reality of the war, in no significant respect had to distort it.

It's possible, however, that Kurtz's monstrosity is intended to be perceived as such, his dubiously Nietszchean ravings taken no more seriously by the director than by a discerning spectator; viewed from this angle, he becomes the perfect product of a highly imperfect system and his only fault has been to take that system's methods and values to their logical conclusion. But since the institutionalized violence of the military — of a Kilgore, for example — is already sufficiently documented in the movie to make Willard wonder how it could be surpassed, what need is there for Kurtz's presence at all?

The ambiguity of Coppola's intentions is further underlined by the weight given the character, not only by the casting of Brando (at a fabulous and much-publicized salary) but by the inordinate degree of suspense generated before we are finally permitted to see him. Led through the compound littered with mutilated corpses and heads on pikes into the confines of the ruined temple, Willard finds himself in a room heavy with stale sweat, sperm, blood, incense and, presumably, Kurtz's own complex vibrations. A few moments pass. Out of the shadows the dome of a bald head slowly materializes. (Another of the film's visual motifs: Brando's baldness, the temple statues, Chef's head tossed into Willard's lap, Willard's head surfacing from the primeval swamp as he prepares to kill Kurtz and, at the very beginning, superimposed upside-down on one of his own nightmares). Kurtz quotes from T. S. Eliot's *The Hollow Men* while massaging the scalp of his (hollow) pate. He ruminates about his Midwestern home. In a rather too artfully composed still-life shot, his bedside reading is exhibited: Jesse L. Weston's *From Ritual to Romance,* Sir James Frazer's classic study of magic and religion, *The Golden Bough,* obviously designed as pointers to guide the spectator toward a true understanding of his impending assassination. For when Willard at last 'terminates' Kurtz, the act is intercut with the ritualized felling of an ox, thus taking on overtones of parricide, both Oedipal and anthropological, the killing of the father, the destitution of a chief whose ebbing powers demand that he willingly sacrifice himself in favor of a younger, stronger man.

But these mythic resonances never seem more than 'token', planted mainly to bolster a sagging narrative, an impression reinforced by Coppola's visible uncertainty as to how the film should end. We know that it was screened in various degrees of rough cut to friends and other movie makers throughout the period of 1978-79; that the version shown at the 1979 Cannes Film Festival (where it won the Palme d'Or *ex aequo* with Volker Schlöndorff's *The Tin Drum*) was even then by no means the definitive one; that Coppola shot, then staggeringly ditched, a mighty ground-and-air assault on Kurtz's base by both American and Viet Cong forces, a final cataclysmic sequence that he hoped would fully justify the movie's title, and that he subsequently reinstated it in the 35mm version intended for general release. That none of these has proved satisfactory — the 70mm ending makes nonsense of the imagery of sacrifice; the 35mm ending provides just one more big bang; the potentially intriguing (if predictable) notion of Willard's morbid obsession with Kurtz toppling over into emulation would require that their relationship be considerably less sketchy than at present — can be ascribed in part to the failure of Brando's Kurtz (and the dialogue written for him) to live up to the promise of his powerful offscreen presence. But it is also symptomatic, in a curious way, of what went terribly askew with the undertaking from the start.

If for much of its length *Apocalypse Now* captures as no other film has done the unprecedented *obscenity* of the Vietnam war, this is due not only to Coppola's unquestioned *savoir faire,* the almost foolhardy boldness of his conception or the hugeness of the budget he was ready to allocate to his mammoth pet project. The very real sense of hopelessness that permeates the movie, the sense of things getting out of hand, of *escalation,* would appear to have derived as much from its difficult shooting conditions (as chronicled — fitfully, alas — by Coppola's wife in her *Notes*) as from the nature of the material itself.

Though it would be irresponsible to carry the comparison too far, one is struck by a number of correspondences between the war and this epic that set out to record it: the legendary investments of time and money swallowed up in the jungle, the invasion of an underdeveloped country by massive Yankee technology, the fuzziness of motivation, the daily battling with the elements, the sense of a journey undertaken which would end no-one knew where, even the reluctance of many of Hollywood's top actors to commit themselves to what promised to be a lengthy location schedule in the Philippines — behaving like so many draft dodgers. When Eleanor Coppola describes her family's provisory return home to the Napa Valley in California after a typhoon had caused the production to be closed down, it's as if she were speaking about a furlough. Martin Sheen has attested to the fact that (almost like a traumatized vet) he was a changed man after the movie. And Coppola, in interviews, admitted that he had

'This is the Way the World Ends, Not With a Bang but a Whimper'. - Kurtz quotes from T.S. Eliot's. 'The Hollow Men'.

begun to identify first with Willard, then with Kurtz (a role in which, for the Hollywood establishment, the installation of his renegade independent company in San Francisco had already cast him).

It's not surprising, then, that he too was defeated in the end by the intricate network of motives, aspirations and blindly pursued objectives to which the term 'Vietnam' had come to be affixed. Coppola's error was to believe — so soon, at least, after the cessation of hostilities — that these could simply be strained out of the experience, leaving only a residue of 'tragic grandeur' to serve as the backdrop for a meditation on the eternal verities of good and evil. What *is* surprising, however, is the extent to which his defeat seemed to mirror that of the whole American entanglement in South-East Asia and thus could be considered almost a fit conclusion to what was always a doomed enterprise.

In the scale of its ambitions, the movie which *Apocalypse Now* most resembles is *2001 – A Space Odyssey* and it may well set a style in filming the war as Kubrick's did for the exploration of space. One critic remarked of *2001* that any science fiction movie hoping to better it would have to be shot *on location.* And the same is perhaps true of *Apocalypse Now* – if by 'on location' we mean that it must be made by the Vietnamese themselves.

Willard emerges from the steaming primeval swamp in preparation for Kurtz's sacrifice.

FILMOGRAPHY

SAIGON

USA 1947 95mins
PARAMOUNT

Producer: P. J. Wolfson
Director: Leslie Fenton
Photography: John Seitz
Screenplay: P. J. Wolfson, Arthur Sheekman based on a story by Julian Zimet
Music: Robert E. Dolan
Cast: Alan Ladd, Veronica Lake, Douglas Dick

Black and White

A YANK IN INDOCHINA

USA 1952 67mins
COLUMBIA

Producer: Sam Katzman
Director: Wallace A. Grissell
Photography: William Whitley
Screenplay: Samuel Newman
Music: Rossi di Maggio
Editor: Aaron Stell
Cast: John Archer, Douglas Dick, Jean Willes, Maura Murphy, Harold Fong

JUMP INTO HELL

USA 1955 92mins
WARNER BROS

Producer: David Weisbart
Director: David Butler
Photography: Peverell Marley
Screenplay: Irving Wallace
Editor: Irene Mora
Music: David Buttolph
Cast: Jack Sernas, Kurt Kaszner, Arnold Moss, Peter Van Eyck, Pat Blake

Black and White

CHINA GATE

USA 1957 90mins
20TH CENTURY FOX/GLOBE ENTERPRISES

Producer: Samuel Fuller
Director: Samuel Fuller
Photography: Joseph Biroc
Screenplay: Samuel Fuller
Editor: Gene Fowler Jnr
Music: Victor Young, Max Steiner
Cast: Gene Barry, Angie Dickinson, Paul Dubov, Nat 'King' Cole, Lee Van Cleef, George Givot

Cinemascope - Black and White

THE QUIET AMERICAN

USA 1957 122mins
UNITED ARTISTS/FIGARO INC.

Producer: Joseph L. Mankiewicz
Director: Joseph L. Mankiewicz
Photography: Robert Krasker
Screenplay: Joseph L. Mankiewicz (based on the novel by Grahame Greene)
Music: Mario Nascimbene
Editor: William Hornbeck
Cast: Audie Murphy, Michael Redgrave, Claude Dauphin, Bruce Cabot, Georgia Moll

Black and White

FIVE GATES TO HELL

USA 1959 89mins
20TH CENTURY FOX

Producer: James Clavell
Director: James Clavell
Photography: Sam Leavitt
Screenplay: James Clavell
Editor: Harry Gerstad
Music: Paul Dunlap
Cast: Dolores Michaels, Neville Brand, Patricia Owens, Ken Scott,

Nancy Kulp Cinemascope - Black and White

BRUSHFIRE

USA 1961 77mins
PARAMOUNT/OBELISK PRODUCTIONS

Producer: Jack Warner Jnr
Director: Jack Warner Jnr
Photography: Edward Fitzgerald
Screenplay: Irwin R. Blacker
Editor: Roy Livingston
Music: Irving Gertz
Cast: John Ireland, Everett Sloane, Jo Morrow
Black and White

THE UGLY AMERICAN

USA 1962 120mins
UNIVERSAL-INTERNATIONAL

Producer: George Englund
Director: George Englund
Photography: Clifford Stine
Screenplay: Stewart Stern (based on the novel by W. J. Ledever and Eugene Burdick)
Music: Frank Skinner
Editor: Ted J. Kent.
Cast: Marlon Brando, Eiji Okada, Pat Hingle, Arthur Hill, Jocelyn Brando, Sandra Church
16 35mm Technicolor/Eastmancolor

A YANK IN VIET-NAM

USA 1963 80mins
ALLIED ARTISTS

Producer: Wray Davis
Director: Marshall Thompson
Photography: Emmanuel Rojas
Screenplay: Jane Wardell and Jack Lewis (from latters story)
Music: Richard Lasalle
Editor: Basil Wrongell and Orver Schanzer
Cast: Marshall Thompson, Enrique Magalona, Mario Bari, Kieu Chinh, Urban Drew, Donald Sealy, Hoang Vinhhoc

LOST COMMAND

USA 1965 130mins
COLUMBIA/RED LION

Producer: Mark Robson
Director: Mark Robson
Photography: Robert Surtees
Screenplay: Nelson Gidding (based on the novel 'The Centurions' by Jean Larteguy
Music: Franz Waxman
Editor: Dorothy Spencer

Cast: Anthony Quinn, Alain Delon, George Segal, Claudia Cardinale, Michelle Morgan, Maurice Ronet

16 35mm Technicolor/Panavision

OPERATION CIA

USA 1965 77mins
(U.S. Last Message from Saigon)
ALLIED ARTISTS/WARNER-PATHE/HEI RA MATT

Producer: Peer J. Oppenheimer
Director: Christian Nyby
Photography: Richard Moore
Screenplay: Bill Ballinger and Peer J. Oppenheimer from the latters original story.
Music: Paul Dunlap
Editor: Joseph Gluck/George Watters
Cast: Burt Reynolds, Danielle Aubry, Kieu Chinh, John Hoyt

16 35mm Technicolor

TO THE SHORES OF HELL

USA 1965
PARADE PICTURES/ZENS/PATRICK PRODUCTION

Producer: Will Zens
Director: Will Zens
Photography: Leif Rise
Screenplay: Robert McFadden and Will Zens
Music: William Schaeffer
Cast: Marshall Thompson, Richard Jordahl, Jeff Pearl, Kiwa Lawrence, Richard Arlen

Technicolor

THE BORN LOSERS

USA 1967 114mins (GB 90mins)
AMERICAN INTERNATIONAL PIC/FOCUS

Producer: Donald Henderson
Director: T. C. Frank (Tom Laughlin)
Photography: Gregory Sandor
Screenplay: E. James Lloyd
Editor: John Wineld
Cast: Tom Laughlin, Elizabeth James, Jane Russell, Jeremy Slate, William Wellman Jnr, Paul Bruce

Pathe Color

WINDFLOWERS

USA 1967 75mins
FILMMAKERS DIST CENTER/WIND FLOWERS CO.

Producer: Adolfas Mekas
Director: Adolfas Mekas
Screenplay: Adolfas Mekas
Music: Adolfas Mekas and Pola Chapelle

Editor: Adolfas Mekas
Cast: John Kramer, Pola Chapelle, Ronnie Gilbert, Henry Calvert, William Taylor

THE ANGRY BREED

USA 1968 88mins
C.U.E./COMMONS/GOLDMAN ASSOCIATES

Producer: David Commons
Director: David Commons
Screenplay: David Commons
Cast: Jan Sterling, James MacArthur, Jan Murray, Murray MacLeod, William Windom

Color

THE BIG BOUNCE

USA 1968 102mins
WARNER/GREENWAY PRODUCTIONS

Producer: William Dozier
Director: Alex March
Photography: Howard. R. Schwartz
Screenplay: Robert Dozier (from the novel by Elmore Leonard)
Music: Michael Curb
Editor: William Ziegler
Cast: Ryan O'Neal, Leigh Taylor-Young, Van Heflin, Lee Grant, James Daly

Panavision/Technicolor

THE EDGE

USA 1968 100mins
BLUE VAN PRODUCTIONS/ALPHA 60

Producer: Robert Kramer, Robert Machover
Director: Robert Kramer
Photography: Robert Machover
Screenplay: Robert Kramer
Editor: Robert Machover
Cast: Jack Rader, Tom Griffin, Howard Loeb Babeuf, Jeff Weiss, Anne Woldman Warsch, Sanford Cohen, Paul Hultberg, Catherine Merrill, Russell Parker

THE GREEN BERETS

USA 1968 141mins
WARNER/BATJAC

Producer: Michael Wayne
Director: John Wayne/Ray Kellogg
Photography: Winton C. Hoch
Screenplay: James Lee Barrett
Editor: Otho Lovering
Music: Miklos Rozsa
Cast: John Wayne, David Janssen, Jim Hutton, Aldo Ray, Raymond St.

Jacques, Jack Soo, Bruce Cabot, Patrick Wayne, Irene Tsu, Jason Evers, Luke Askew

Panavision/Technicolor

GREETINGS

USA 1968 88mins (GB 85mins)
EAGLE/WEST END FILMS

Producer: Charles Hirsch
Director: Brian Di Palma
Photography: Robert Fiore
Screenplay: Charles Hirsch/Brian Di Palma
Music: The Children of Paradise
Editor: Brian Di Palma
Cast: Robert De Niro, Jon Warden, Gerritt Graham, Megan McCormick Ashley Oliver

Eastmancolor

ALICE'S RESTAURANT

USA 1969 110mins
UNITED ARTISTS/FLORIN

Producer: Hillard Elkins/Joe Manduke
Director: Arthur Penn
Photography: Michael Nebbia
Screenplay: Venable Herndon and Arthur Penn (based on the 'Alice's Restaurant Massacree' by Arlo Guthrie)
Music: Garry Sherman
Editor: Dede Allen
Additional Music: 'Songs to ageing Children' *by Joni Mitchell;* 'Pastures of Plenty' and 'Car Song' *by Woody Guthrie*
Cast: Arlo Guthrie, Pat Quinn, James Broderick, Michael McClanathan, Geoff Outlaw

Technicolor De Luxe

EASY RIDER

USA 1969 95mins
COLUMBIA/PANDO/RAYBERT

Producer: Peter Fonda
Director: Dennis Hopper
Photography: Lazlo Kovacs
Screenplay: Peter Fonda, Dennis Hopper, Terry Southern,
Editor: Donn Cambren
Cast: Peter Fonda, Dennis Hopper, Phil Spector, Antonio Mendoza, Jack Nicholson

Technicolor

Music: *Steppenwolf:* 'The Pusher'and 'Born to be Wild'; *The Band:* 'The Weight'; *The Byrds:* 'I Wasn't born to follow'; *Little Eva:* 'Let's Turkey trot'; *Jimi Hendrix experience:* 'If Six Was Nine'; *The Electric Prunes:* 'Kyrie Eleision'; *The Electric Flag:* 'Flash, Bam, Pow'; *The Holy Model Rounders:* 'If You Want to be a Bird'; *Fraternity of Man:* 'Don't Bogart Me'; *Roger McGuinn:* It's alright Mama (I'm only bleeding) and 'Ballad of Easy Rider'

HAIL, HERO

USA 1969 97mins (GB 88mins)
EMI/WARNER PATHE

Producer: Harold D. Cohen.
Director: David Miller
Photography: Robert Hauser
Screenplay: David Manber (from the novel by John Weston)
Music: Jerome Moross
Editor: Jack McSweeney
Songs: Gordon Lightfoot
Cast: Michael Douglas, Arthur Kennedy, Teresa Wright, John Larch, Charles Drake, Mercer Harris

Technicolor

HI, MOM!

USA 1969 87mins
WEST END FILMS

Producer: Charles Hirsch
Director: Brian De Palma
Photography: Robert Elfstrom
Screenplay: Brian De Palma (from a story by De Palma and Hirsch)
Music: Eric Kaz
Editor: Paul Hirsch
Cast: Robert De Niro, Charles Durnham, Allen Garfield
Songs: *Jeffrey Lesser:* 'Hi Mom!'; *Boney Srabian:* 'I'm Looking at You'; *Grady Tate:* 'Me Black' all written by *Eric Kaz, J. Andreoli*

16mm Color

M*A*S*H*

USA 1969 115mins
20TH CENTURY FOX/ASPEN INC.

Producer: Ingo Preminger
Director: Robert Altman
Photography: Harold E. Stine
Screenplay: Ring Lardner Jnr (based on the novel by Richard Hooker)
Music: Johnny Mandel
Editor: Danford B. Greene
Song: 'Suicide is Painless' by *Johnny Mandel and Mike Altman*
Cast: Donald Sutherland, Elliott Gould, Robert Duvall, Tom Skeritt Sally Kellerman, Jo Ann Pflug, Gary Burghoff

Panavision/De Luxe

MEDIUM COOL

USA 1969 111mins
PARAMOUNT/H & J PICTURES

Producer: Tully Friedman
Director: Haskell Wexler
Photography: Haskell Wexler
Screenplay: Haskell Wexler
Editor: Verna Fields

Music: Mike Bloomfield
Incidental music: *Mothers of Invention* 'Merry Go Round' by *Wild Man Fisher*
Cast: Robert Forster, Verna Bloom, Peter Bonerz, Marianna Hill, Sid McCoy

Technicolor

SATAN'S SADISTS

USA 1969 86mins
INDEPENDENT INT/KENNIS-FRAZER

Producer: Al Adamson
Director: Al Adamson
Photography: Gary Graver
Screenplay: Dennis Wayne
Editor: Gary Graver
Music: Harley Hatcher performed by *'The Nightriders'*
Cast: Russ Tamblyn, Scott Brady, Kent Taylor, John Carlos, Robert Dix, Gary Kent

De Luxe

ZABRISKIE POINT

USA 1969 112mins
MGM

Producer: Carlo Ponti
Director: Michelangelo Antonioni
Photography: Alfio Contini
Screenplay: Antonioni, Fred Garner, Sam Shepard, Tonio Guerra, Clare Peploe
Editor: Franco Arcalli (Assistant)
Music: *Pink Floyd:* 'Kaleidoscope'; *Jerry Garcia* and *John Fahey:* 'Dance of Death'; *Grateful Dead:* 'Dark Star'; *Rolling Stones:* 'You Got the Silver'; *The Youngbloods:* 'Sugarbabe'; *Patti Page:* 'Tennessee Waltz'; *Roscoe Holcomb:* 'I wish I were a Single Girl again' - Electronic Effects by *Music Electronics Viva*
Cast: Mark Frechette, Rod Taylor, Daria Halprin, Paul Fix

Panavision/Metrocolor

THE MODEL SHOP

USA 1969 92 mins
COLUMBIA

Producer: Jacques Demy
Director: Jacques Demy
Screenplay: Jacques Demy
Photography: Michael Hugo
Editor: Walter Thompson
Music: Spirit
Cast: Anouk Aimée, Gary Lockwood, Alexandra Hay, Carol Cole

Technicolor

COWARDS

USA 1970 89mins
JAYLO INTERNATIONAL

Producer: Lewis Mishkin and Simon Nuchtern
Director: Simon Nuchtern
Photography: Robert T. Megginson
Screenplay: Simon Nuchtern
Editor: Robert T. Megginson
Music: Stephen Lerner performed by *'The Merry-Go-Round'*
Cast: John Rose, Susan Sparling, Will Patent, Thomas Murphy

Eastmancolor

GETTING STRAIGHT

USA 1970 125mins
COLUMBIA/THE ORGANIZATION

Producer: Richard Rush
Director: Richard Rush
Photography: Laszlo Kovacs
Screenplay: Robert Kaufman (based on the novel by Ken Kolb)
Music: Ronald Stein
Editor: Maury Winetrobe
Cast: Elliott Gould, Candice Bergen, Robert Lyons, Jeff Corey, Max Julien, Cecil Kellaway

Eastmancolor

THE HARD RIDE

USA 1970 90mins
MGM-EMI/American Int

Producer: Charles Hanawalt
Director: Burt Topper
Photography: Robert Sparks
Screenplay: Burt Topper
Editor: Kenneth Crane
Music: Harley Hatcher
Songs: *The Arrows:* 'Grady's Bunch'; *Bill Medley:* 'Swing Low Sweet Chariot'; *Junction:* 'Falling in love with Baby'; *Bob Moline:* 'Where am I going'; *Thelma Camacho:* 'I came along to be with you' and 'Carry Me Home'; *Paul Wibier:* 'Be Nobody's Fool', 'Let the Music Play', 'Shannon's Hook Shop' and 'Another Kind of War'
Cast: Robert Fuller, Sherry Bain, Marshall Reed, William Bonner

Color by Movielab

HOMER

USA 1970 90mins
WARNER-PATHE/EDGAR PRODUCTIONS

Producer: Terry Dene and Steve North
Director: John Trent
Photography: Lazlo George

Screenplay: Claude Harz
Editor: Michael Manne
Music: Don Scardino
Cast: Don Scardino, Tisa Farrow, Alex Nicol, Lenka Peterson, Ralph Enderby, Trudy Young

Technicolor

ICE

USA 1970 132mins
AFI/MONUMENT FILM CORPORATION

Producer: David Stone
Director: Robert Kramer
Photography: Robert Machover
Screenplay: Robert Kramer

Black and White

JOE

USA 1970 106mins
BRITISH LION/CANNON PRODUCTIONS

Producer: David Gil
Director: John Avildson
Photography: John Avildson
Screenplay: Norman Wexler
Editor: George Norris
Music: Bobby Scott
Cast: Peter Boyle, Susan Sarandon, Dennis Patrick
Songs: *Dean Michaels:* 'Hey Joe'; *Exuma:* 'You don't know what's going on'; *Jerry Butler:* 'Where are you going' and 'You can fly'

De Luxe

THE REVOLUTIONARY

USA 1970 101mins
UNITED ARTISTS/PRESSMAN-WILLIAMS

Producer: Edward Pressman
Director: Paul Williams
Photography: Brian Probyn
Screenplay: Hans Koningsberger
Editor: Henry Richardson
Music: Michael Small
Cast: Jon Voight, Jennifer Salt, Robert Duvall, Seymour Cassel, Collin Wilcox-Horne

Technicolor

THE STRAWBERRY STATEMENT

USA 1970 109mins
MGM

Producer: Irwin Winkler and Robert Chartoff
Director: Stuart Hagmann

Photography: Ralph Woolsey
Screenplay: Israel Horovitz (based on the novel by James Kunen)
Music: Ian Freebairn-Smith
Editor: Marje Fowler, Fredric Steinkamp and Roger Roth
Cast: Bruce Davison, Kim Darby, Bud Cort, Murray MacLeod, Israel Horovitz
Songs: *Buffy Saint-Marie:* 'The Circle Game'; *Thunderclap Newman:* 'Something in the Air'; *Crosby, Stills, Nash and Young:* 'Helpless', 'Our House' and 'Suite Judy Blue Eyes'; *Neil Young:* 'The Loner' and 'Down by the River'; *Lennon:* 'Give Peace a Chance'

Metrocolor

JUD

USA 1971 80mins
MARON FILMS/DUQUE FILMS

Producer: Igo Kantor
Director: Gunther Collins
Photography: Isidare Mankojsky
Screenplay: Gunther Collins
Music: Stu Phillips
Song: *Bob Dylan:* 'One too Many Mornings'
Cast: Joseph Kaufmann, Robert Demon, Alix Wyeth, Claudia Jennings, Maurice Sherbanee

Movielab Color

THE LOSERS

USA 1971 95mins
MGM-EMI

Producer: Joe Soloman
Director: Jack Starrett
Photography: Nonong Rasca
Screenplay: Alan Caillou
Music: Stu Phillips
Editor: James Moore & Richard Brockway
Cast: William Smith, Bernie Hamilton, Adam Rourke, Houston Savage, Paul Koslo, Gene Cornelius

Eastmancolor

PRISM

USA 1971 80mins
CORN KING FILMS

Producer: Bob Silverstein, Jay Freund and Anitra Pivnick
Director: Anitra Pivnick
Photography: Jay Freund
Screenplay: Anitra Pivnick
Music: Tom Manoff
Editor: Jay Freund, Anitra Pivnick
Cast: Paul Greier, Dale Soules, Nancy Volkman, Ozzi Tortora, Frank Geraci

Du Art Color

BILLY JACK

USA 1971 113mins
WARNER/NATIONAL STUDENT FILM CORPORATION

Producer: Mary Rose Solti
Director: T.C. Frank (Tom Laughlin)
Photography: Fred Koenekamp, John Stephens
Screenplay: Tom Laughlin and Delores Taylor
Music: Mundell Lowe
Editor: Larry Heath and Marian Rothman
Cast: Tom Laughlin, Delores Taylor, Bert Freed, Clark Howat, Julie Webb, Ken Tobey, Victor Izay

Technicolor

CHROME AND HOT LEATHER

USA 1971 95mins
AMERICAN INTERNATIONAL

Producer: Wes Bishop
Director: Lee Frost
Photography: Lee Frost
Screenplay: Michael Haynes, David Neibel and Don Tait (story by Haynes and Neibel)
Music: Porter Jordan
Editor: Alfonso La Mostra and Edward Shryver
Cast: William Smith, Tony Young, Michael Haynes, Peter Brown, Marvin Gaye, Michael Stearns

Movielab color

GLORY BOY

USA 1971 103mins
(G.B. MY OLD MAN'S PLACE)
CINERAMA/WAXMAN-MINSKOFF PRODUCTIONS

Producer: Phillip A. Waxman
Director: Edwin Sherin
Photography: Richard C. Glouner
Screenplay: Stanford Whitmore (based on the novel by John Sanford)
Music: Charles Gross(Norma Green)
Editor: Ferris Webster
Cast: Arthur Kennedy, Michael Moriarty, Mitchell Ryan, Topo Swope, William Devane

Eastmancolor

SUMMERTREE

USA 1971 89mins
COLUMBIA/WARNER/BRYNA

Producer: Kirk Douglas
Director: Anthony Newley
Photography: Richard Glouner
Screenplay: Edward Hume and Stephen Yafa (based on the play by

Ron Cowen)
Music: David Shire
Editor: Maury Winetrobe
Song: 'Having the time of our lives' by *Shire* and *Maltby*
Cast: Michael Douglas, Jack Warden, Brenda Vaccaro, Barbara Bel Geddes, Kirk Callaway, Bill Vint

Eastmancolor

TAKING OFF

USA 1971 92mins
UNIVERSAL

Producer: Alfred Crown and Michael Houseman
Director: Milos Forman
Photography: Gordon Lang
Screenplay: Milos Forman, John Guare, John Klein, and Jean Claude Carrière
Editor: John Carter
Cast: Lynn Carlin, Buck Henry, Linnea Heacock, Ike and Tina Turner
Songs: *Nina Hart:* 'Love'; *Susan Chafitz:* 'Fields of Green and Gold'; *Mike Leander, Eddie Seago:* 'Lets get a little sentimental'; *Bobo Bates:* 'Even the Horses had wings'; *Carly Simon:* 'Long Term effects'; *Tom Eyen and Peter Cornell:* 'Ode to a Screw'; *Cathy Heriza:* 'Lessons in love'; *Tchaikovsky:* 'Nocturne'; *Ike and Tina Turner:* 'Goodbye, Solong'; *Mike Turner (Incredible String Band):* 'Air'; *Caren Klugman:* 'Feeling sort of Nice'; *Dvorak:* 'Stubat Mater' No 58'

Movielab Color

CLAY PIGEON

(G.B. Trip to Kill)
USA 1971 93mins
TRACOM/DOVERTON (G.B.)

Producer: Tom Stern
Photography: Alan Stensvold
Director: Tom Stern
Screenplay: Ronald Buck, Buddy Ruskin and Jack Gross Jnr (from a story by Buddy Ruskin and Jack Gross Jnr)
Music: Gavin Murrell
Editor: Danford Greene
Cast: Telly Savalas, Tom Stern, Robert Vaughn, Peter Lawford, Burgess Meredith, Mario Alcalde, James Dobson

Metrocolor

F.T.A.

USA 1972 96mins
FREE THEATER ASSOCIATES

Producer: F. Parker, Jane Fonda, Donald Sutherland
Director: Francine Parker
Photography: Juliana Wang, Eric Saarinen, John Weidman
Screenplay: Michael Alaimo, Len Chandler, Pamela Donegan, Jane Fonda, Rita Martinson, Robin Menken, Holly Near, Don Sutherland, Dalton Trumbo
Editor: Joel Moorwood, Michael Beaudry

Cast: Jane Fonda, Donald Sutherland, Pamela Donegan, Len Chandler, Rita Martinson, Michael Alaimo
Songs FTA: *Len Chandler:* 'My Ass is mine', 'Move on over' and 'Set the date'; *Robin Menken:* 'Nothing could be finer than to be in Indochina', 'So nice to be a member of the Military Class' and 'Save our Soldiers'; *Rita Martinson:* 'Soldier we love you'; *Kinturozn:* 'Broken Island, Broken Home'; *Homer Swann:* 'A Brand new day'; *Beverley Grant:* 'I'm tired of those Bastards Fucking me over'; *Uncredited:* 'Fox-trot, Tango, Alpha'
Choreography: Sylvia Walden

16mm Color

LIMBO

USA 1972 111mins
UNIVERSAL/FILMMAKERS/ORANGE OMAHA

Producer: Linda Gottleib
Director: Mark Robson
Photography: Charles Wheeler
Screenplay: Linda Gottleib and Joan Silver (from their novel)
Music: Anita Kerr
Editor: Dorothy Spencer
Cast: Kate Jackson, Kathleen Nolan, Katherine Justice, Russell Wiggins, Hazel Medina

Technicolor

OUTSIDE IN

USA 1972 90mins
HAROLD ROBBINS INT

Producer: George Edwards
Director: Allan Brown
Photography: Mario Tosi
Screenplay: Robert Hutchinson (based on story by Hutchinson and Baron)
Music: Randy Edelman
Cast: Darrel Larson, Heather Menzies, Dennis Olivieri, John Bill, Peggy Feury, Logan Ramsey

De Luxe Color

PARADES

USA 1972 95mins
CONFRON PRODUCTIONS

Producer: Robert J. Siegel
Director: Robert J. Siegel
Photography: Saul Negrin
Screenplay: George Tabori
Music: Gary Sherman
Editor: Richard Marks
Cast: Russ Thacker, Brad Sullivan, Lewis J. Stadler, David Doyle, Dorothy Chace

De Luxe Color

SLAUGHTER

USA 1972 90mins
A.I.P/SLAUGHTER UNITED

Producer: Monroe Sachson
Director: Jack Starrett
Photography: Rosanio Solano
Screenplay: Mark Hanna and Don Williams
Music: Luchi de Jesus
Editor: Renn Reynolds
Cast: Jim Brown, Rip Torn, Don Gordon, Cameron Mitchell

De luxe Todd-Ao 35mm

THE TRIAL OF THE CATONSVILLE 9

USA 1972 85mins
MELVILLE PRODUCTIONS

Producer: Gregory Peck
Director: Gordon Davidson
Photography: Haskell Wexler
Screenplay: Daniel Berrigan, Saul Levitt (based on play by Daniel Berrigan)
Music: Shelly Manne
Editor: Aaron Stell
Cast: Gwen Arner, Ed Flanders, Barton Heyman, Richard Jordan, Nancy Malone, Davis Roberts

Eastmancolor

THE VISITORS

USA 1972 90mins
ASSOCIATED ARTISTS

Producer: Chris Kazan, Nick Proferes
Director: Elia Kazan
Photography: Nick Proferes
Screenplay: Chris Kazan
Music: *Bach:* Suite No1 for Lute, *William Matthews:* guitar
Editor: Nick Proferes
Cast: Patrick McVey, Patricia Joyce, Chico Martinez, James Woods, Steve Railsback

Color

WELCOME HOME, JOHNNY BRISTOL

USA 1972 120mins (GB 90mins)
CBS TV/CINEMA CENTER

Producer: Arthur Joel Katz
Director: George McCowan
Screenplay: Stanley Greenberg
Cast: Martin Landau, Brock Peters, Forrest Tuckers, Martin Sheen, Jane Alexander, Pat O'Brien

Color

WELCOME HOME, SOLDIER BOYS

USA 1972 91mins
20TH CENTURY FOX

Producer: Marvin Schwartz
Director: Richard Compton
Photography: Don Birnkrant
Screenplay: Gordon Trueblood
Music: Ken Wannberg, Ronee Blakely, The Country Gazette
Editor: Patrick Kennedy
Cast: Joe Don Baker, Paul Koslo, Alan Vint, Jennifer Billingsley, Elliott Street

De Luxe Color

AMERICAN GRAFFITI

USA 1973 110mins
UNIVERSAL/LUCASFILM

Producer: Francis Ford Coppola and Gary Kurtz
Director: George Lucas
Photography: Ron Eveslage and Jan D'Alquen
Screenplay: George Lucas, Gloria Lucas and Willard Huyck
Music Coordinator: Karin Green
Editor: Verna Fields and Maria Lucas
Cast: Richard Dreyfuss, Ronny Howard, Paul le Mat, Charlie Martin Smith, Candy Clark, Cindy Williams, MacKenzie Phillips, Wolfman Jack

Technicolor

SUMMER SOLDIERS

JAPAN 1971 103 min
TESHIGAHARA PRODUCTIONS

Producer: Yukio Tomizawa
Director: Hiroshi Teshigahara
Screenplay: John Nathan
Photography: Hiroshi Teshigahara
Editor: Fusako Shuzui

Music: Toru Takemitzu
Cast: Keith Sykes, Lee Reisen, Greg Antonacci, Kazuo Kitamura, Shoichi Ozowa, Tetsuko Kuroyanagi

Color

TWO PEOPLE

USA 1973 100mins
UNIVERSAL/FILMAKERS GROUP

Producer: Robert Wise
Director: Robert Wise
Photography: Henri Decae
Screenplay: Richard De Roy
Music: David Shire
Editor: William Reynolds
Cast: Peter Fonda, Lindsay Wagner, Estelle Parsons, Geoffrey Horne, Alan Fudge

Technicolor

MILESTONES

USA 1975 195 mins
N.Y. CINEMA Co.

Producer: Barbara & David Stone
Director: Robert Kramer & John Douglas
Screenplay: Robert Kramer & John Douglas
Photography: Robert Kramer & John Douglas & Barbara Stone
Editor: Robert Kramer & John Douglas
Music: Bobby Buechler
Cast: Grace Paley, Mary Chapelle, Susie Solf, Paul Zimet Jim Nolfi, John Douglas

Color

TRACKS

USA 1975 92mins
RAINBOW PICTURES

Producer: Howard Zucker
Director: Henry Jaglom
Photography: Paul Glickman
Screenplay: Henry Jaglom
Editor: George Folsey Jnr
Cast: Dennis Hopper, Taryn Power, Dean Stockwell, Topo Swope, Michael Emil, Barbara Flood, Zack Norman, Alfred Ryder
Songs: *Kay Kyser and Orchestra:* 'Praise the Lord and pass the ammunition'; *Dinah Shore:* 'Say it'; *Bing Crosby:* 'These foolish things'; *Tommy Dorsey/Frank Sinatra:* 'This love of mine'; *Kay Kyser:* 'He wears a

pair of Silver wings'; *Carson Robinson:* 'We're going to have to slap that dirty little Jap'; *Jimmy Dorsey and Orchestra:* 'My Sister and I'; *Fred Astaire:* 'The way you look tonight'

TAXI DRIVER

USA 1976 114mins
COLUMBIA/WARNER/BILL PHILLIPS

Producer: Michael and Julia Phillips
Director: Martin Scorsese
Photography: Michael Chapman
Screenplay: Paul Schrader
Music: Bernard Herrmann
Editor: Tom Rolf, Melvin Shapiro
Supervising Editor: Marcia Lucus
Cast: Robert De Niro, Cybill Shepherd, Jodie Foster, Peter Boyle, Harvey Keitel
Songs: *Jackson Browne:* 'Late for the sky'; *George 'oobie' McKen:* 'Hold Me Close'

Metrocolor

THE BOYS IN COMPANY C

Hong Kong 1977 128mins
EMI/RAYMOND CHOW

Producer: Andre Morgan
Director: Sidney Furie
Photography: Godfrey Godar
Screenplay: Rick Natkin
Music: Jaime Mendoza-Nava
Editor: Michael Berman
Song: *Craig Wasson:* 'Here I am'
Cast: Stan Shaw, Michael Lembeck, James Canning, Craig Wasson, Andrew Stevens

Panavision/Technicolor

GOOD GUYS WEAR BLACK

USA 1977 95mins
ENTERPRISE PICTURES LTD

Producer: Allan F. Bodoh
Director: Ted Post
Screenplay: Bruce Cohn and Mark Medoff (from a story by Joseph Fraley)
Music: Craig Safan
Cast: Chuck Norris, Anne Archer, Lloyd Haynes, Dana Andrews, Jim Backus and James Franciscus

CFI Color

HEROES

USA 1977 113mins (G.B. 107)
UNIVERSAL/TURMAN-FOSTER CO

Producer: David Foster and Lawrence Turman

Director: Jeremy Paul Kagan
Photography: Frank Stanley
Screenplay: John Carabatos
Music: Jack Nitzsche
Song: *Kansas:* 'Carry on Wayward Son'
Editor: Patrick Kennedy
Cast: Henry Winkler, Sally Field, Harrison Ford, Val Avery, Olivia Cole

Technicolor

JUST A LITTLE INCONVENIENCE

USA 1977 120mins (G.B. 96mins)
UNIVERSAL T.V./FAWCETT-MAJORS PRODUCTIONS

Producer: Allan Balter
Director: Theodore. J. Flicker
Photography: Duke Callaghan
Screenplay: Theodore J. Flicker and Allan Balter
Music: Jimmy Haskell
Editor: Bernard J. Small
Cast: Lee Majors, James Stacy, Barbara Hershey, Lane Bradbury, Jim Davis

Technicolor

ROLLING THUNDER

USA 1977 99mins (G.B. 94)
AMERICAN INTERNATIONAL PICTURES

Producer: Norman T. Herman
Director: John Flynn
Photography: Jordan Cronenweth
Screenplay: Paul Schrader and Heywood Gould (based on an original story by Paul Schrader)
Music: Barry Devorzon
Editor: Frank P. Keller
Cast: William Devane, Tommy Lee Jones, Linda Haynes, James Best, Luke Askew.

Movielab De Luxe Color

TWILIGHT'S LAST GLEAMING

USA/WEST GERMANY 1977 122mins (U.S. 146)
LORIMAR/BAVARIA STUDIOS

Producer: Merv Adelson
Director: Robert Aldrich
Photography: Robert Hauser
Screenplay: Ronald Cohen and Edward Huebsch (based on the novel by Walter Wager)
Music: Jerry Goldsmith
Editor: Michael Luciano, Maury Winetrobe
Cast: Burt Lancaster, Richard Widmark, Charles Durning, Melvyn Douglas, Paul Winfield, Burt Young, Joseph Cotton, Roscoe Lee Browne

Technicolor

BIG WEDNESDAY

USA 1978 119mins
WARNER BROS/A-TEAM PRODUCTIONS

Producer: Buzz Feitshons
Director: John Milius
Photography: Bruce Surtees,
(surf sequences) Greg MacGillivroy
Screenplay: John Milius and Dennis Aaberg
Music: Basil Poledowis
Editor: Robert Wolfe, Tim O'Meara
Cast: Jan-Michael Vincent, William Kall, Gary Busey, Darrell Fetty.
Songs: *Little Eva:* 'The Locomotion'; *The Crystals:* 'He's a rebel'; *Carole King:* 'Will you love me tomorrow?'; *Four Seasons:* 'Cheri'; *Trini Lopez:* 'La Bamba'; *Booker T and the M.G's:* 'Green Onions'; *Bobby Freeman:* 'Do you want to Dance?'; *Barrett Strong:* 'Money'

Metrocolor/Panavision

COMING HOME

USA 1978 128mins
UNITED ARTISTS/JAYNE PRODUCTIONS INC.

Producer: Jerome Hellman
Director: Hal Ashby
Photography: Haskell Wexler
Screenplay: Waldo Salt and Robert Jones
Songs: *Lennon and McCartney:* 'Hey Jude' and 'Strawberry Fields'; *Deadric Malone:* 'Call on Me'; *Tim Buckley:* 'Once I was'; *Neil Young:* 'Expecting to Fly'; *Stephen Stills:* 'For what its worth'; *Chambers Bros:* 'Time has come today'; *Bob Dylan:* 'Just like a woman'; *Aretha Franklin:* 'Save me'; *Ritchie Havens:* 'Follow'; *Jimi Hendrix:* 'Manic Depression'; *Grace Slick/Jefferson Airplane:* 'White Rabbit'; *Rolling Stones:* 'Out of Time', 'Jumpin Jack Flash', 'No expectations', 'Ruby Tuesday' and 'Sympathy for the Devil'; *Simon and Garfunkel:* 'Bookends'; *Mars Bonfire - Steppenwolf:* 'Born to be Wild'
Editor: Don Zimmerman
Cast: Jane Fonda, Jon Voight, Bruce Dern, Robert Carradine, Robert Ginty.

Metrocolor De Luxe

THE DEER HUNTER

USA 1978 183mins
COLUMBIA/EMI/WARNER

Producer: Barry Spikings, Michael Deeley, Michael Cimino, John Peverall
Director: Michael Cimino
Photography: Vilmos Zsigimond
Screenplay: Michael Cimino, Deric Washburn, Louis Garfinkle, Quinn Redeker
Music: Stanley Myers
Editor: Peter Zinner
Cast: Robert De Niro, John Cazale, John Savage, Christopher Walken, Meryl Streep, George Dzundza, Chuck Aspegren

Panavision/Technicolor

DOG SOLDIERS

(U.S. Who'll Stop the Rain)
USA 1978 124mins
UNITED ARTISTS

Producer: Herb Jaffe, Gabriel Katzka
Director: Karel Reisz
Photography: Richard Kline
Screenplay: Judith Rascoe (from the novel by Robert Stone)
Music: Lawrence Rosenthal
Editor: John Bloom
Cast: Nick Nolte, Michael Moriarty, Tuesday Weld, Anthony Zerbe, Gail Strickland

MGM/Technicolor

FRIENDLY FIRE

USA 1979 180 mins
ABC TV/MARBLE ARCH PRODUCTIONS (STARGER)

Producer: Phillip Barry, Fay Kanin
Director: Harry May
Screenplay: Fay Kanin (based on a true story-book by C. D. B. Bryan)
Cast: Carol Burnett, Ned Beatty, Sam Waterston, Dennis Erdman

Color

GO TELL THE SPARTANS

USA 1978 114mins
UNITED ARTISTS/MAR VISTA

Producer: Alan Bodoh and Mitchell Cannold
Director: Ted Post
Photography: Harry Stradling, Jnr
Screenplay: Wendell Mayes (based on the novel by Daniel Ford)
Music: Dick Halligan
Editor: Millie Moore
Cast: Burt Lancaster, Craig Wasson, Jonathan Goldsmith, Marc Singer, Joe Unger, Dennis Howard

Color

HAIR

USA 1978 120mins
UNITED ARTISTS/CIP PRODUCTIONS

Producer: Lester Persky and Michael Butler
Director: Milos Forman
Photography: Miroslav Ondricek
Screenplay: Michael Weller
Editor: Lynzee Klingman
Music: Galt MacDermott
Lyrics: Gerome Ragni, James Rado
Choreography: Twyla Tharp
Cast: John Savage, Treat Williams, Beverly D'Angelo, Annie Golden, Don Dacus, Dorsey Wright, Suzette Charles, Nicholas Ray

Panavision/Technicolor

APOCALYPSE NOW

USA 1979 35mm 153mins, 70mm 141mins
COLUMBIA/WARNER/EMI/ZOETROPE

Producer: Francis Ford Coppola
Director: Francis Ford Coppola
Photography: Vittorio Storaro
Screenplay: John Milius and Francis Coppola
Music: Carmine and Francis Coppola
Editor: Richard Marks
Cast: Marlon Brando, Robert Duvall, Martin Sheen, Harrison Ford, Dennis Hopper, Sam Bottoms, Frederic Forrest, Albert Hall
Other Music: *The Doors:* 'The End'; *Rolling Stones:* 'I can't get no Satisfaction'; *Robert Duvall:* 'Love me and let me love you'; *Richard Wagner:* 'The Ride of the Valkyries' from 'Die Walkure'; *Leonard Lee:* 'Let the Good times Roll'; *Flash Cadillac:* 'Suzy Q' by Dale Hawkins, S.J. Lewis and E. Broadwater; *Musée de l'homme:* 'Mnong Gar Music from Vietnam – (OCORA Radio France); T.S. Eliot: 'The Hollow Men'

Technovision/Technicolor

A SMALL CIRCLE OF FRIENDS

UNITED ARTISTS/SMALL CIRCLE OF FRIENDS
USA 1980 112 mins

Producer: Tim Zinnemann
Director: Rob Cohen
Screenplay: Ezra Sacks
Photography: Michael Butler
Editor: Randy Roberts
Music: Jim Steinman
Cast: Brad Davis, Karen Allen, Shelley Lacy, Jameson Parker, John Freidrich

Technicolor